HAPPY ST. PATRICK'S DAY

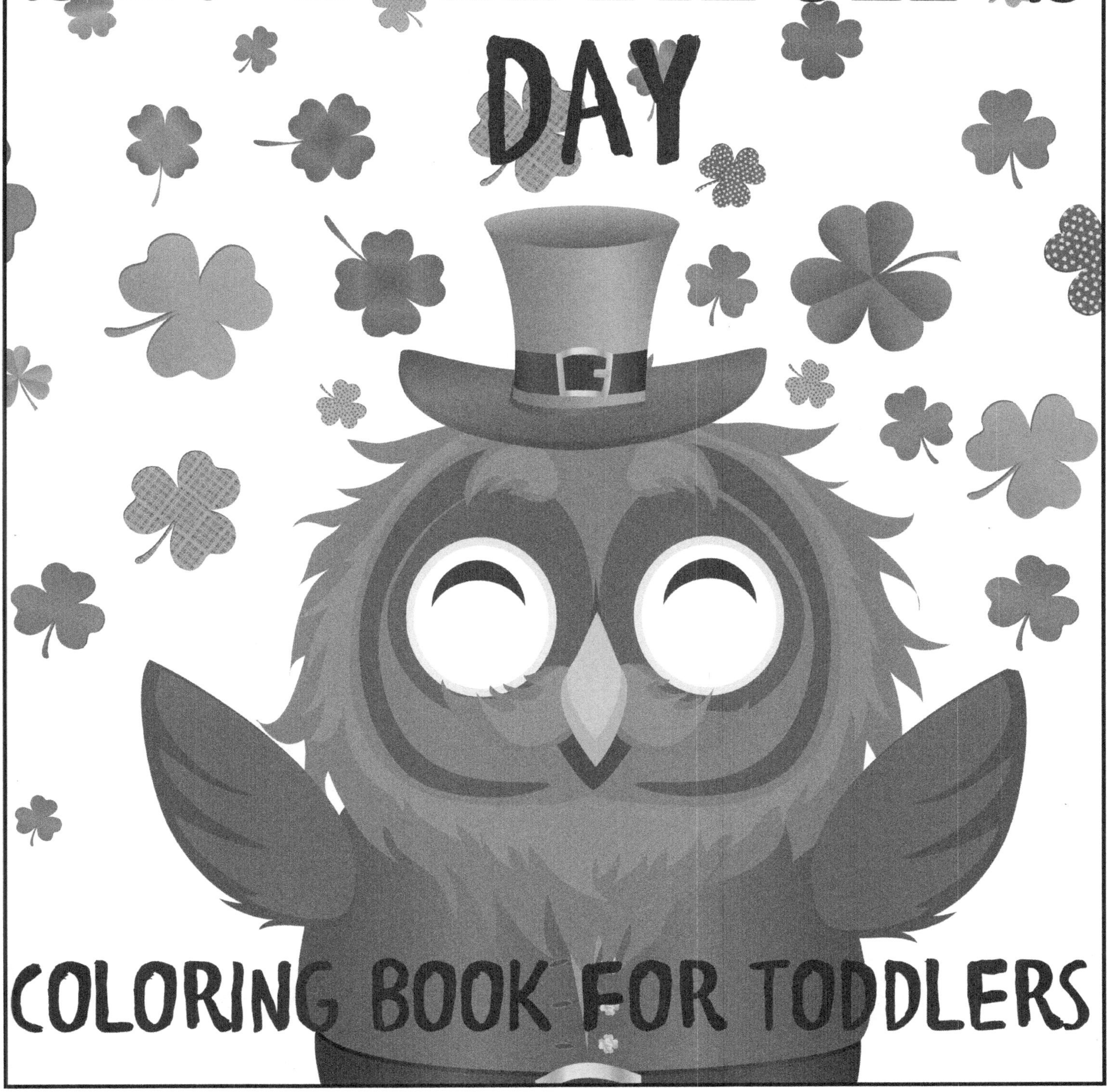

COLORING BOOK FOR TODDLERS

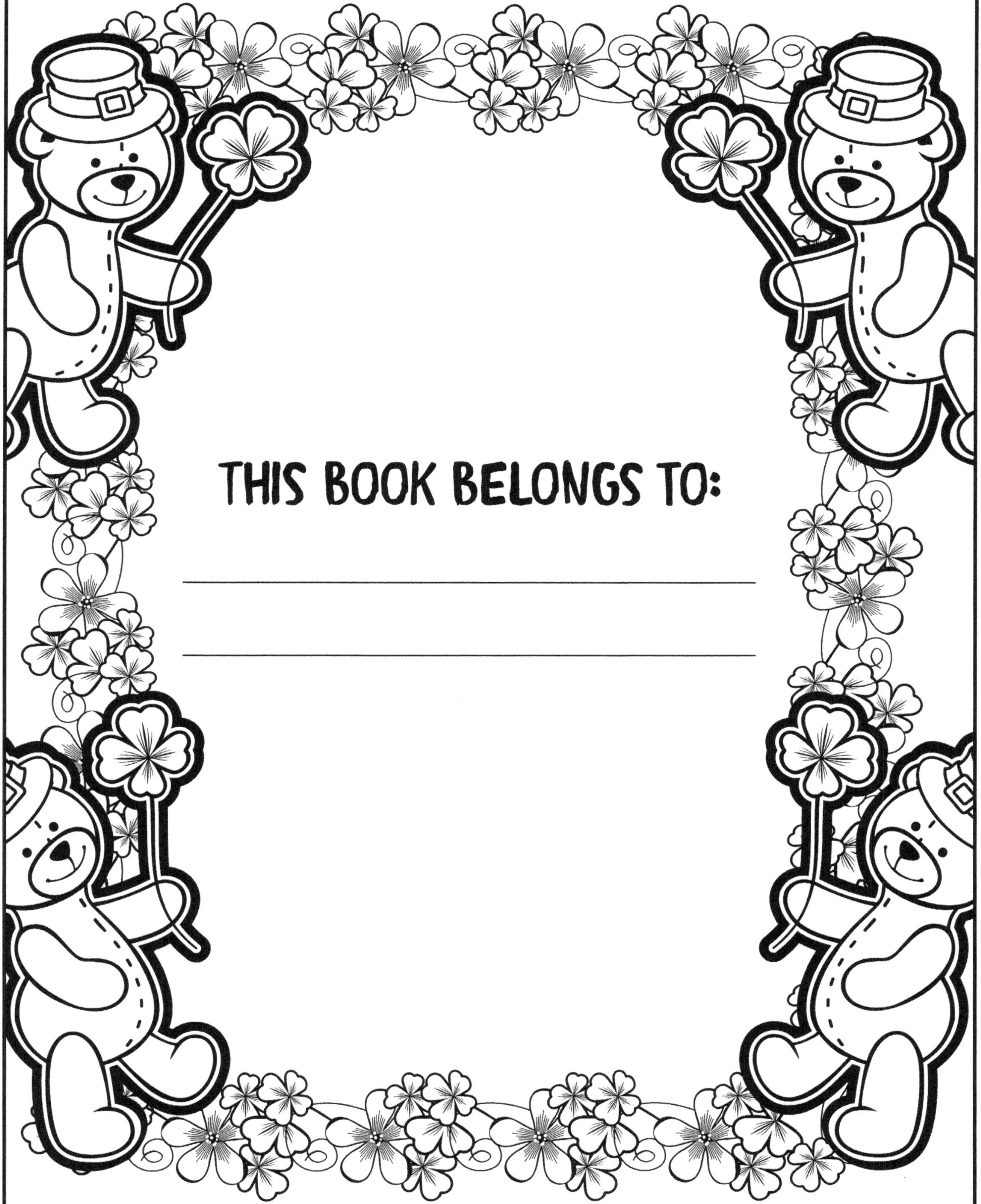

THIS BOOK BELONGS TO:

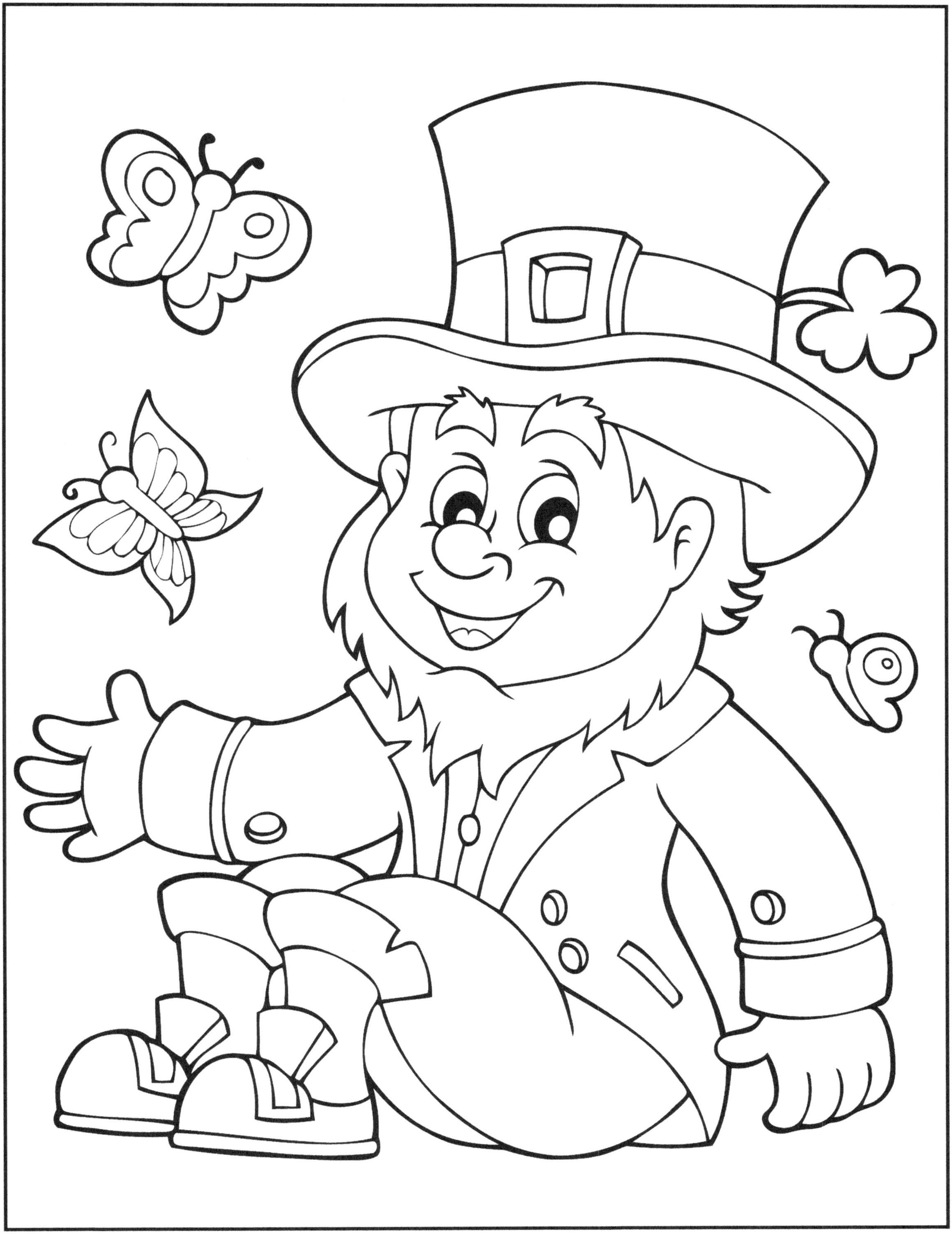

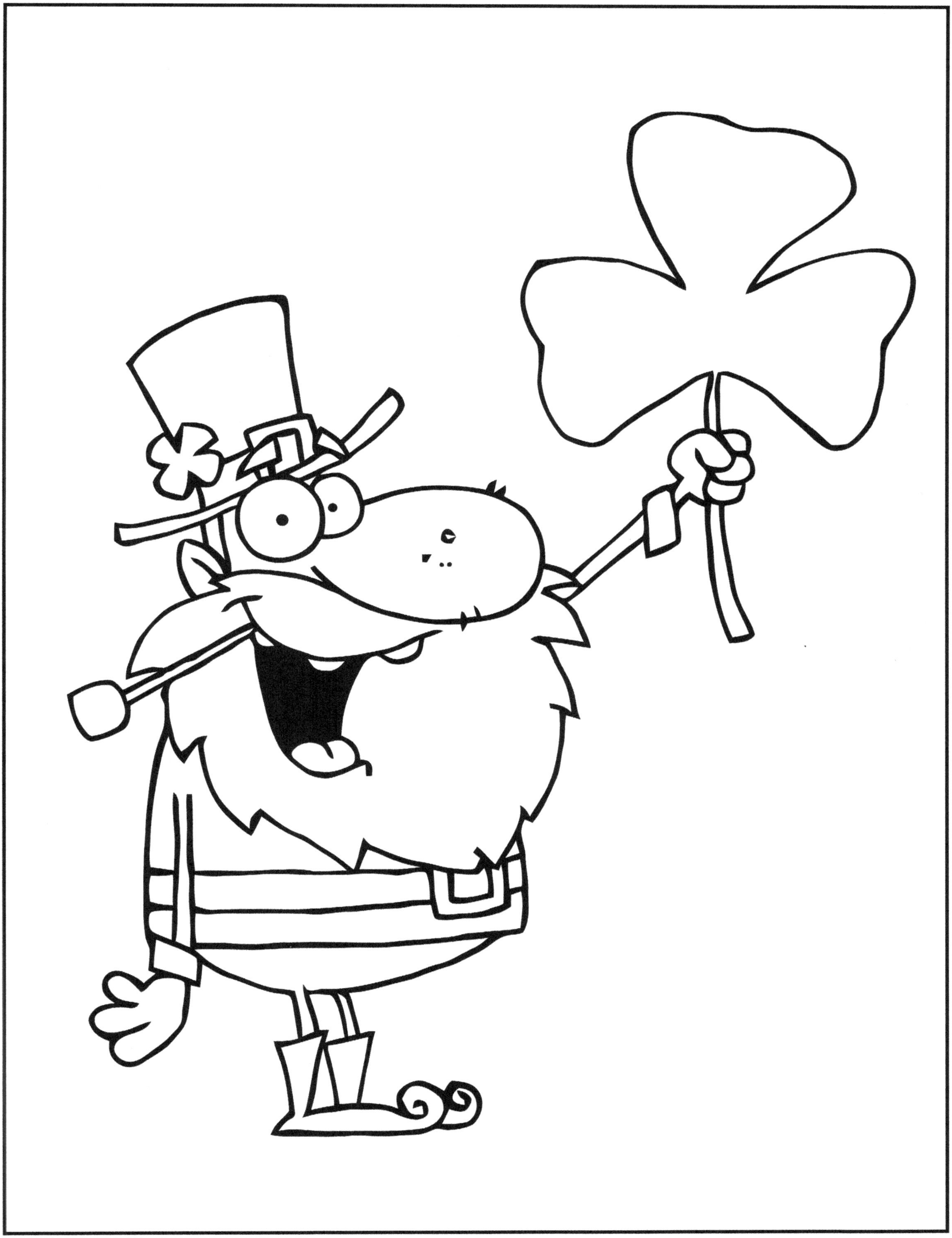

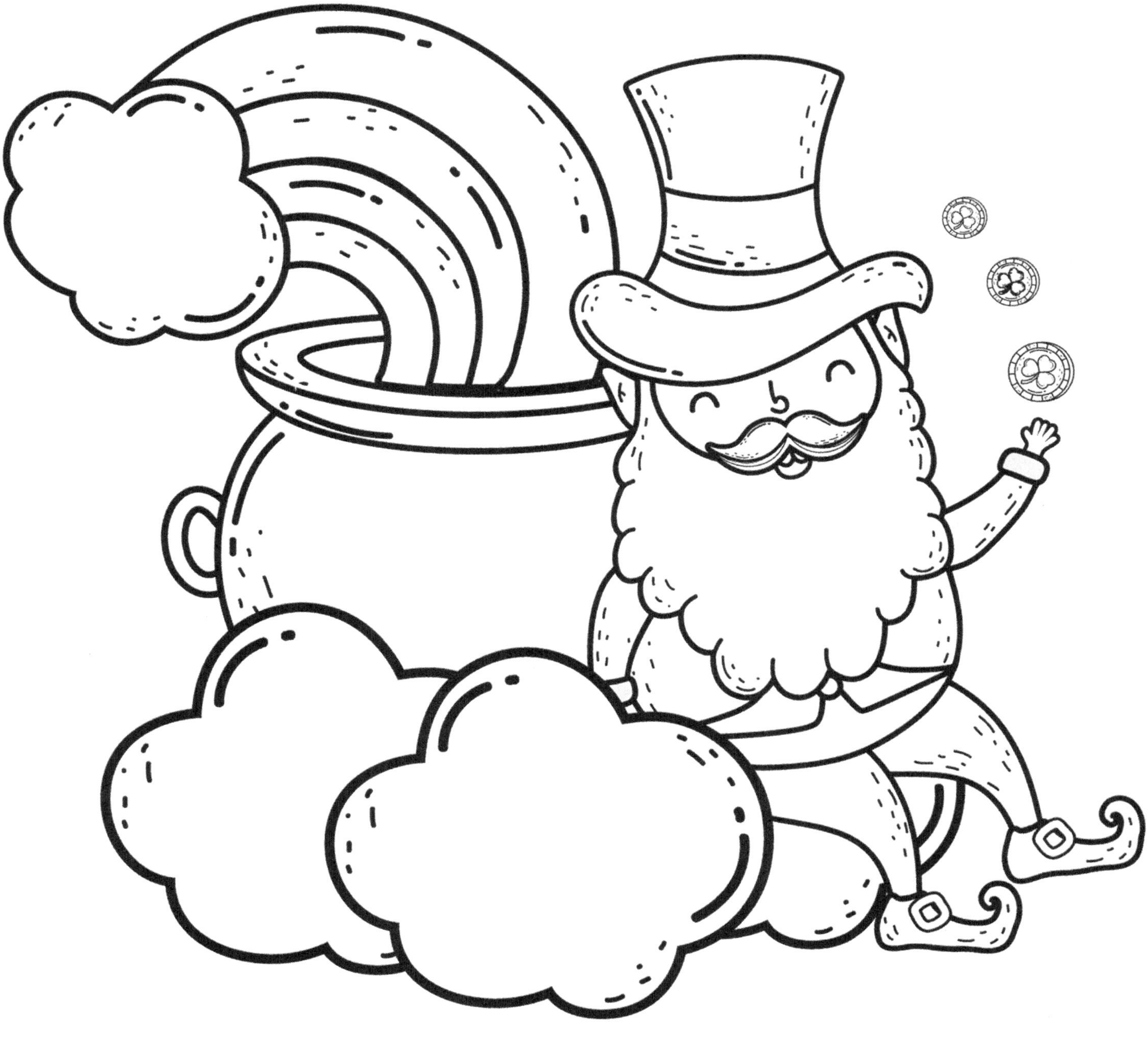

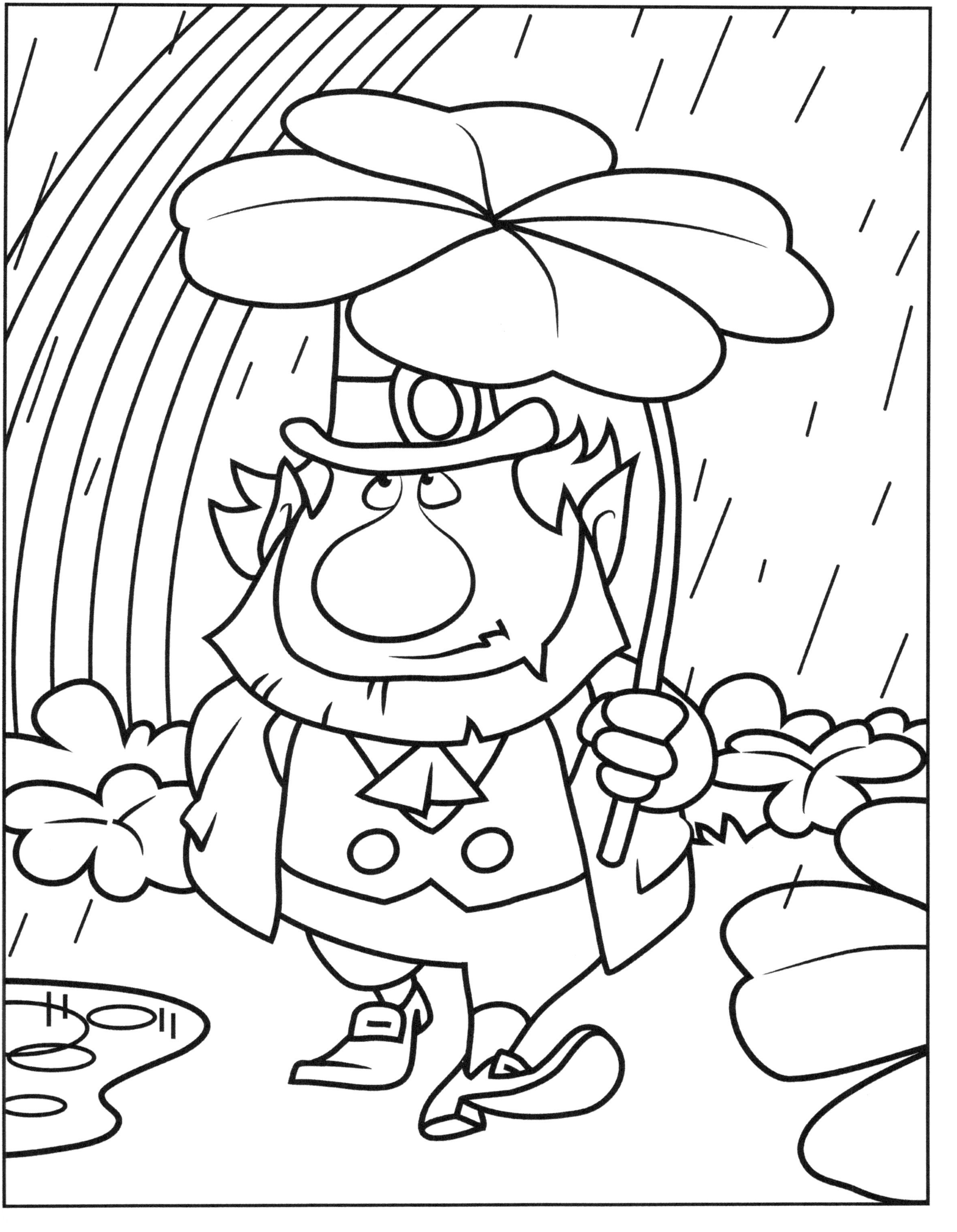

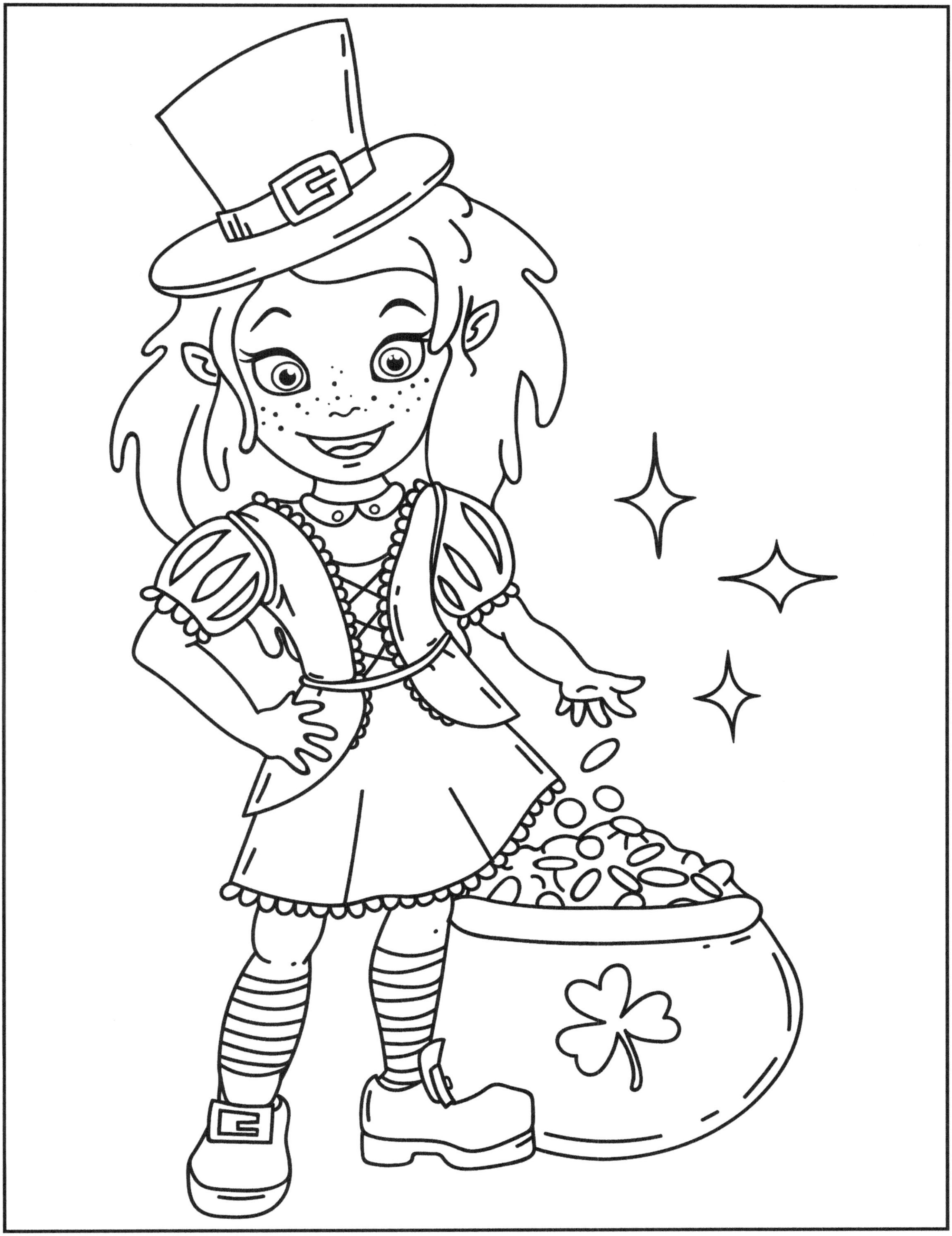

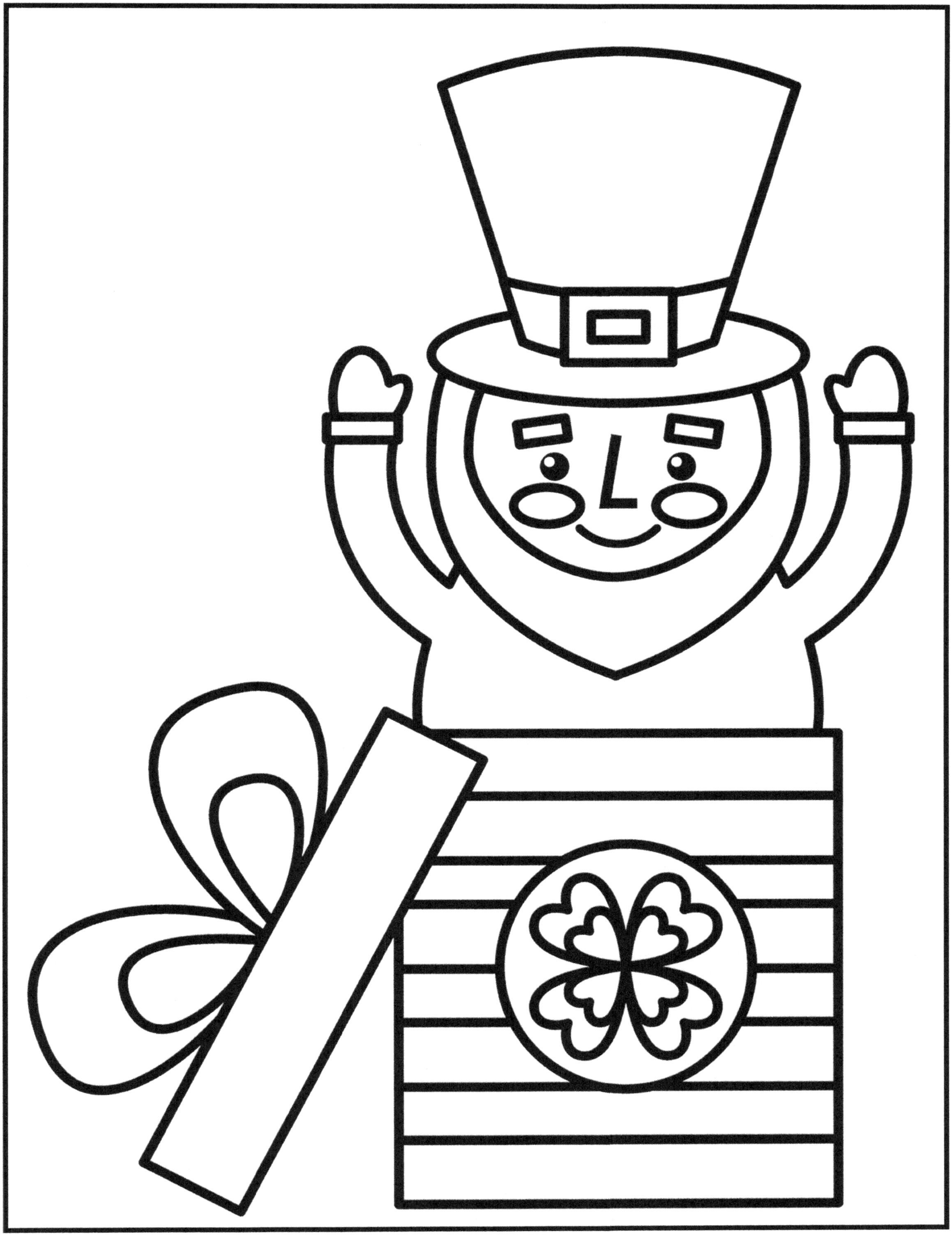

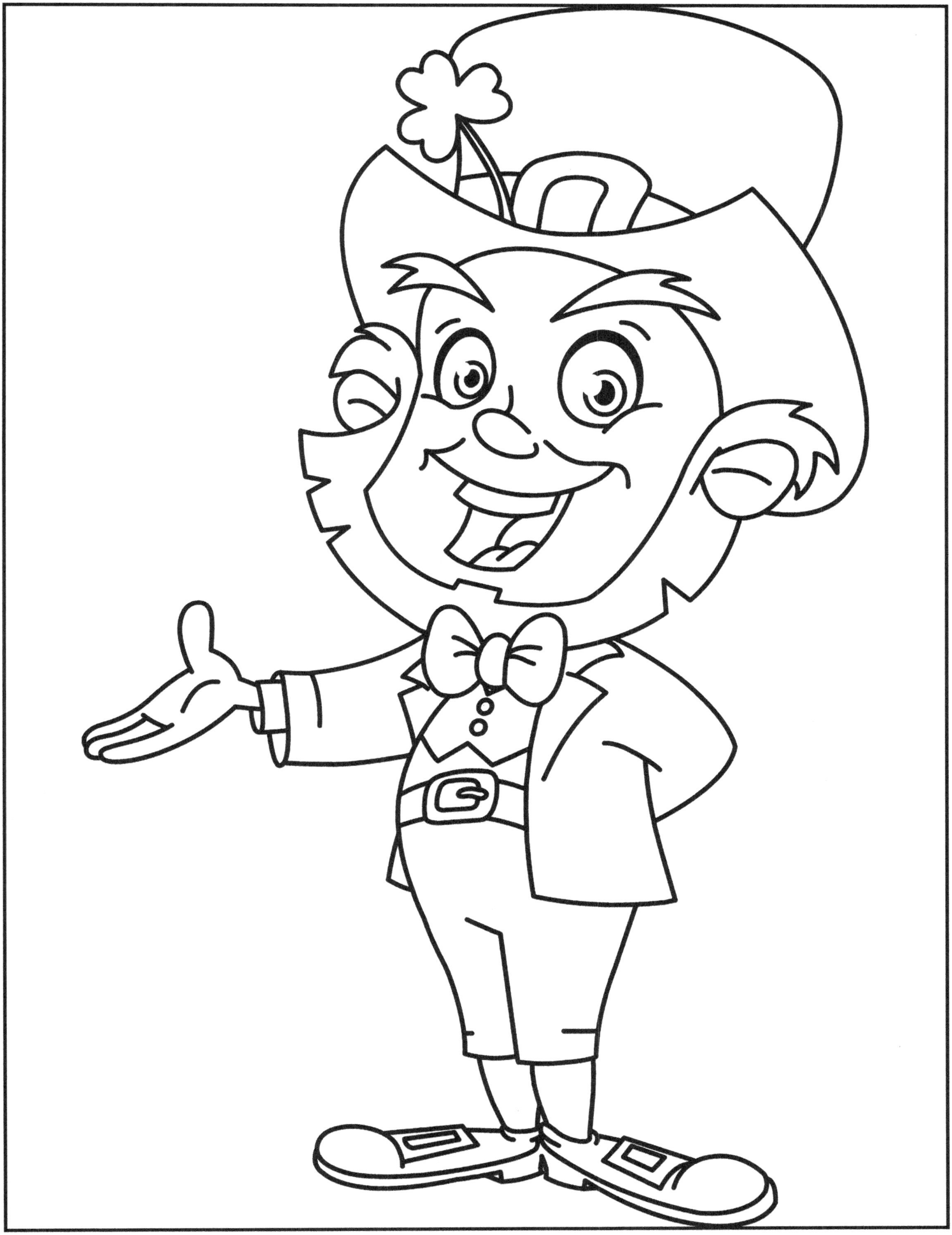

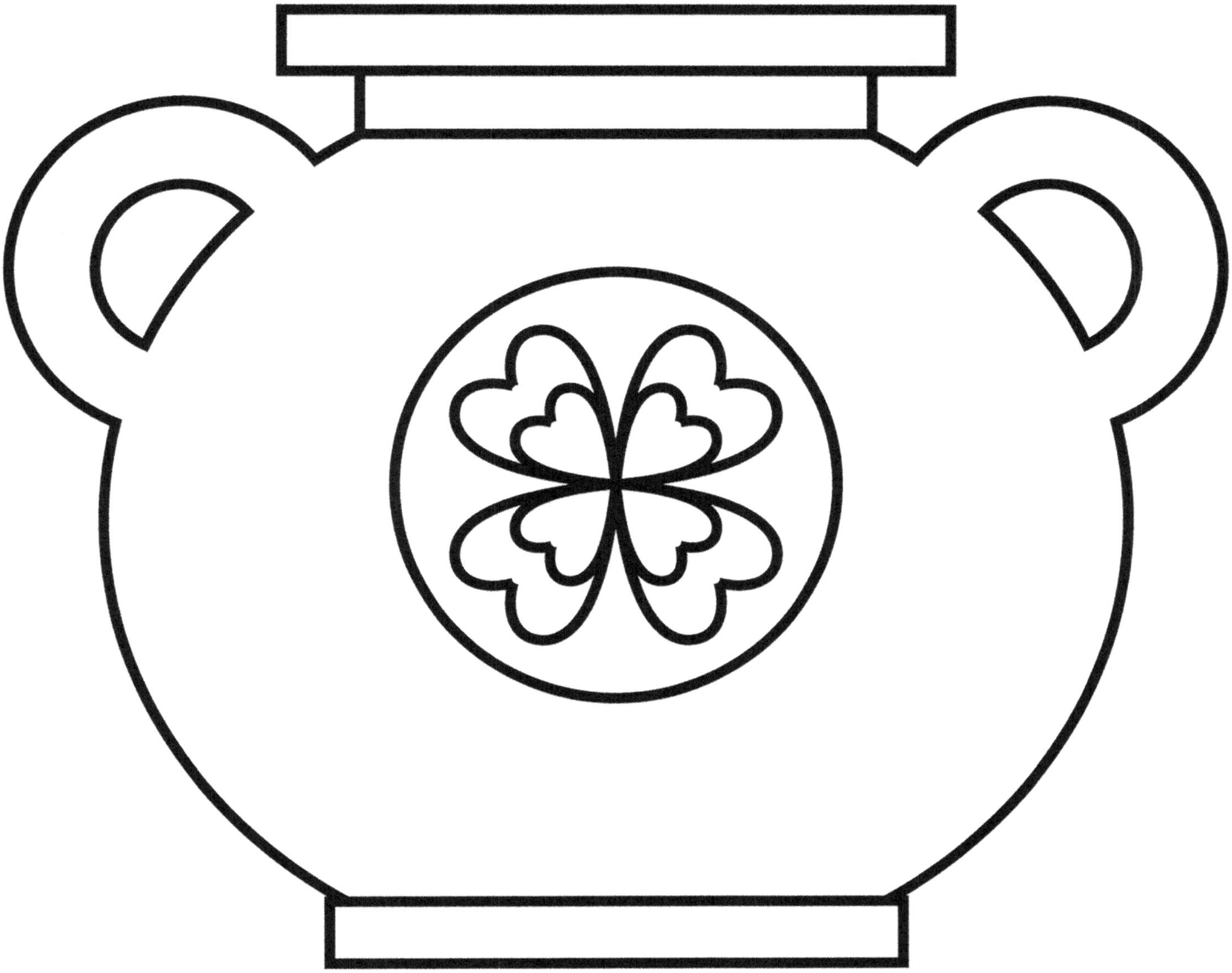

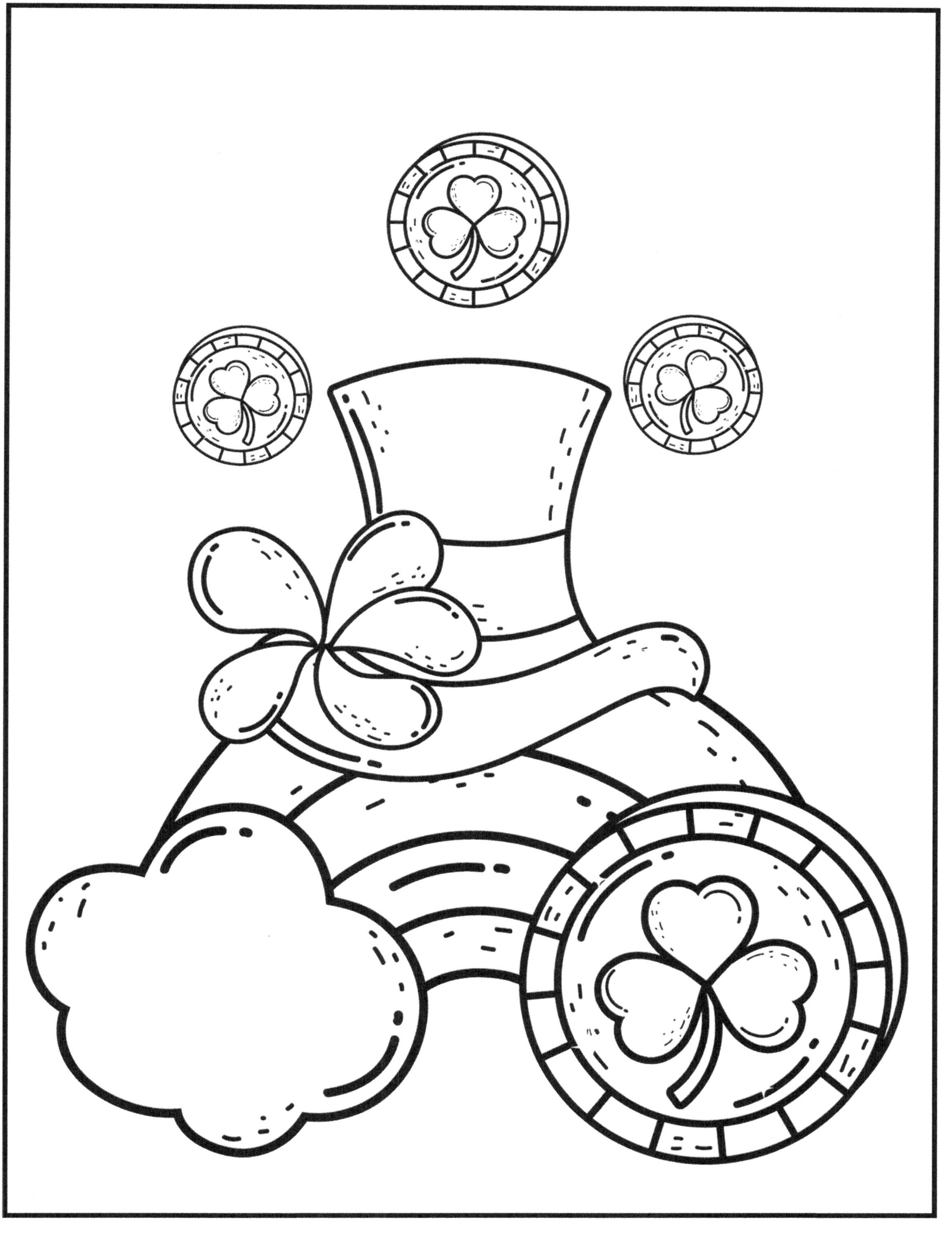

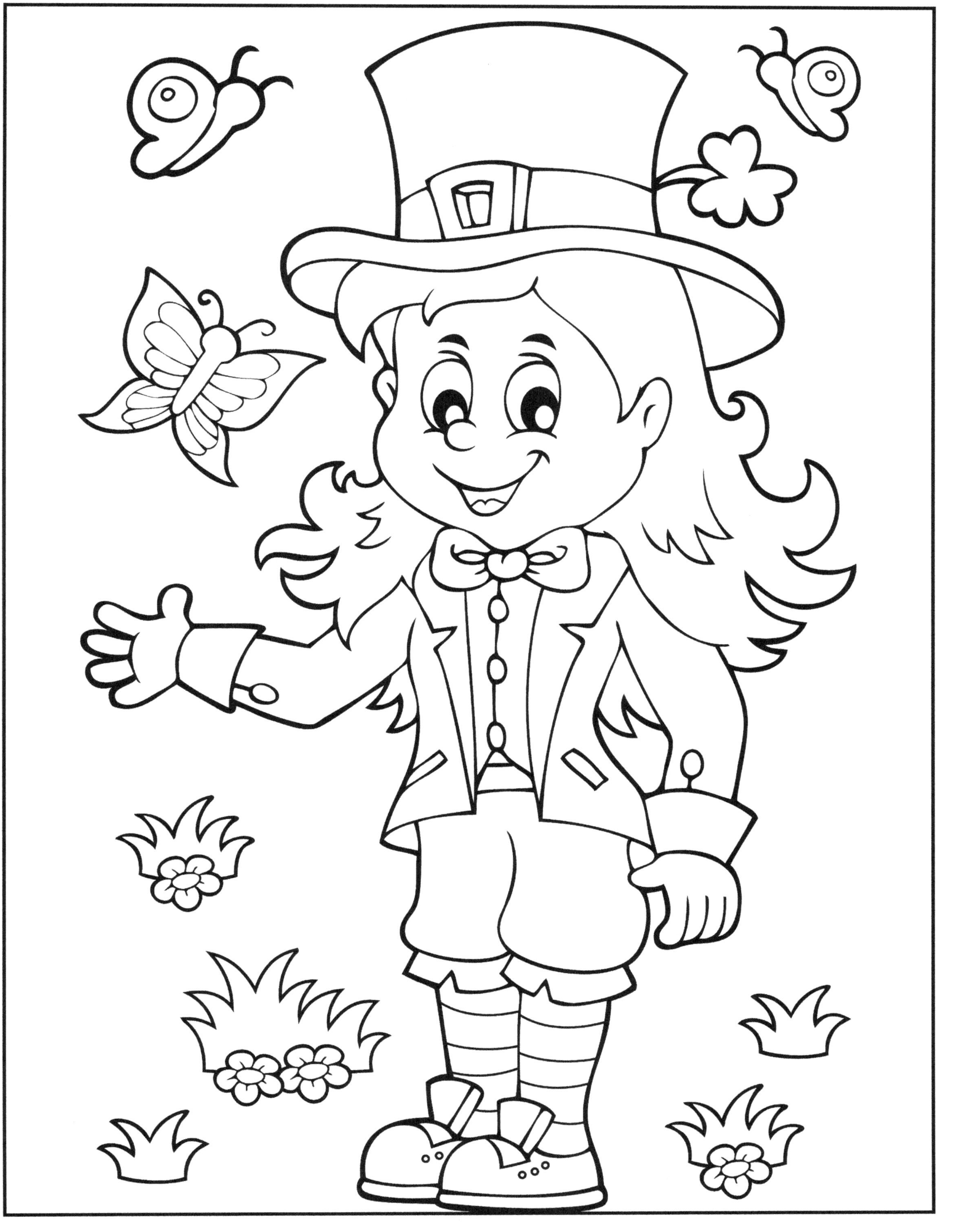

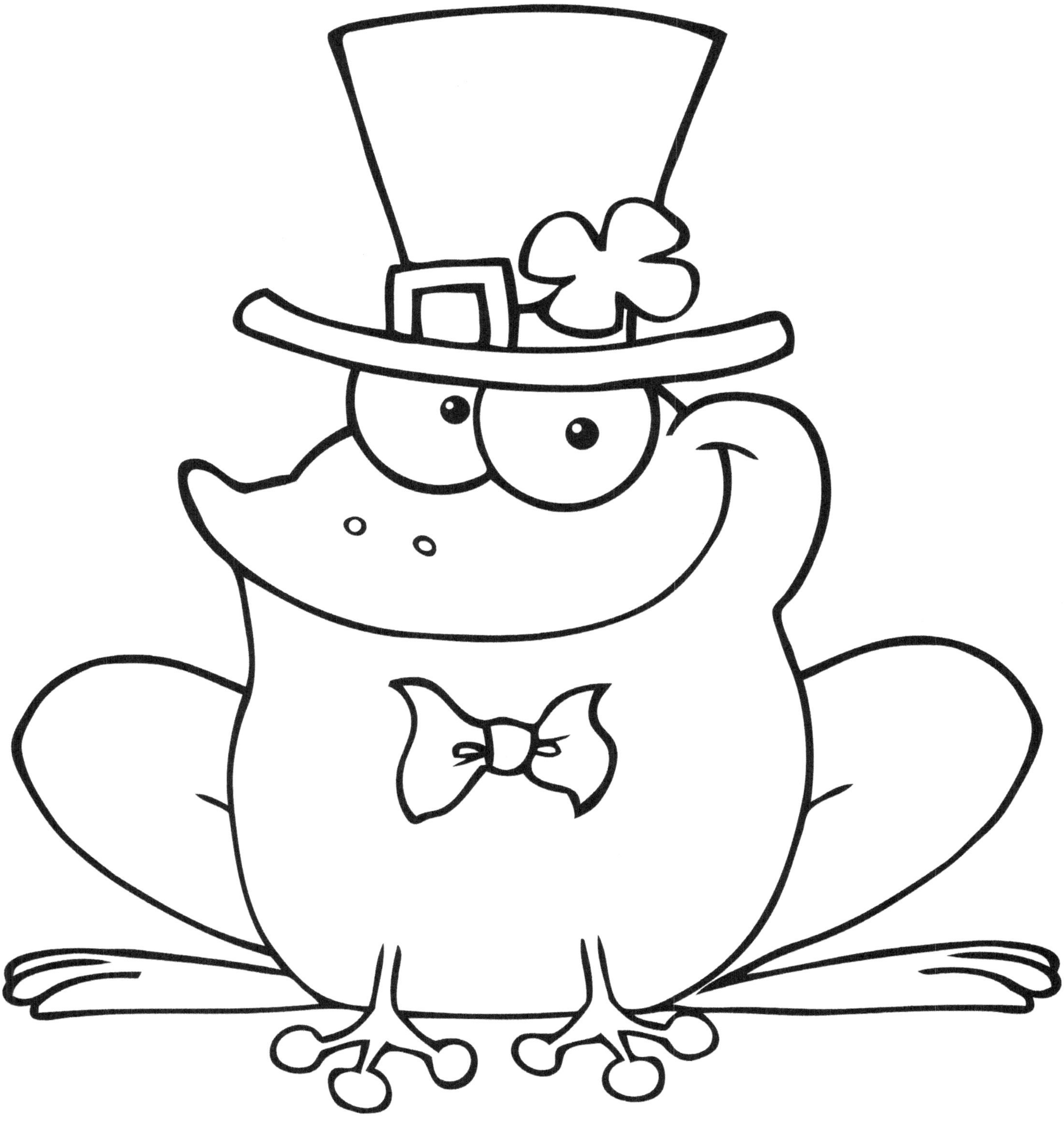

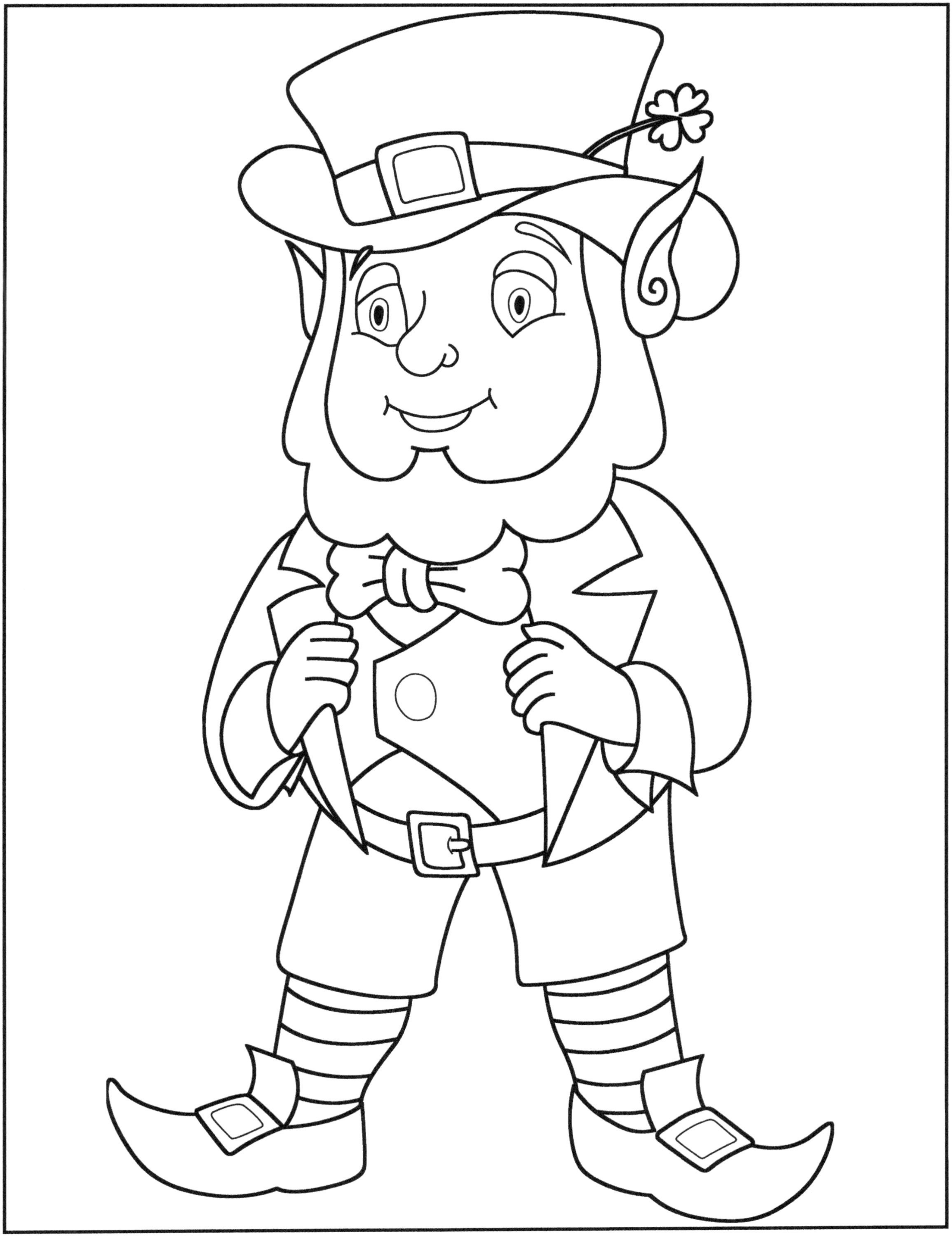

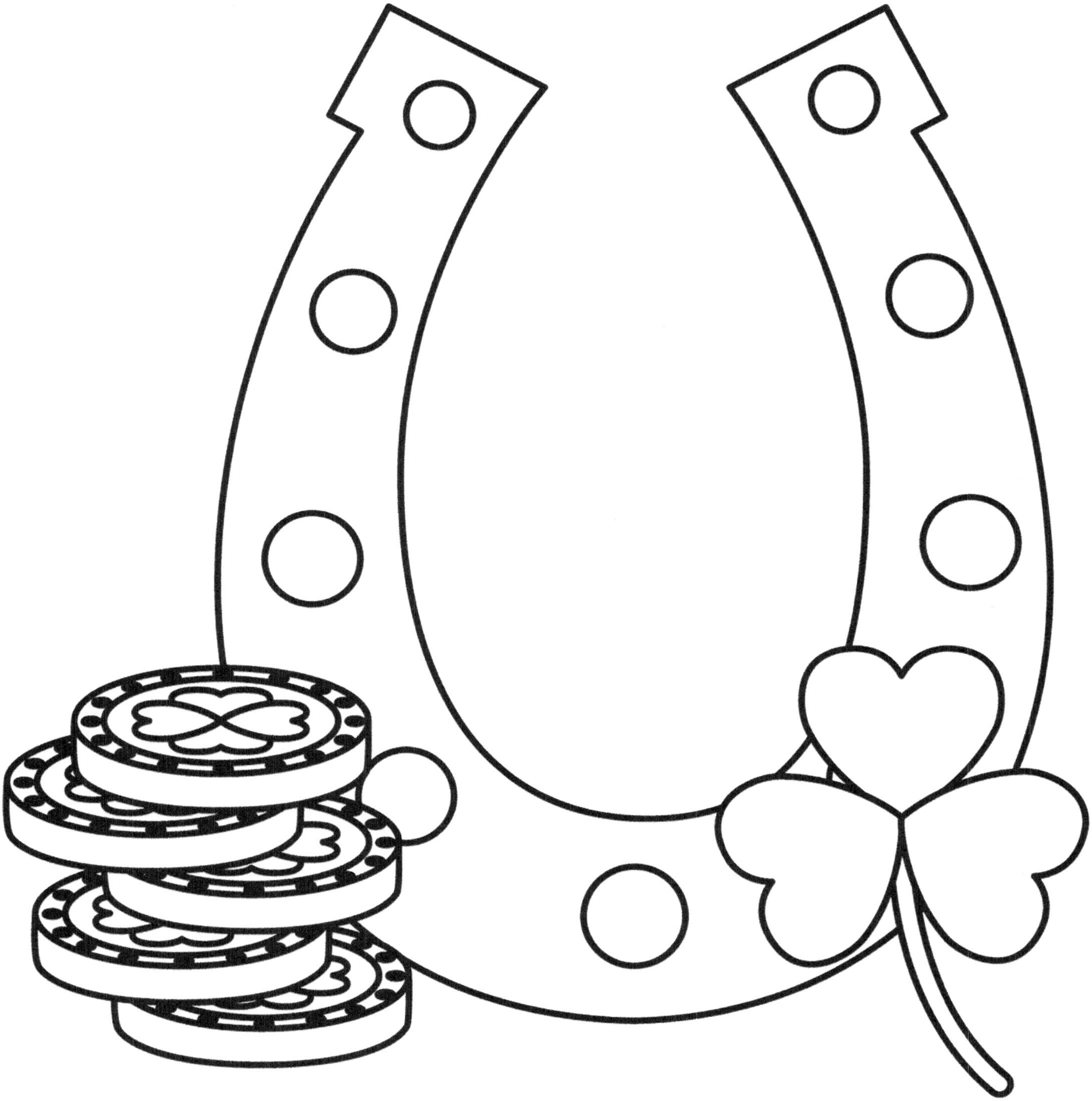

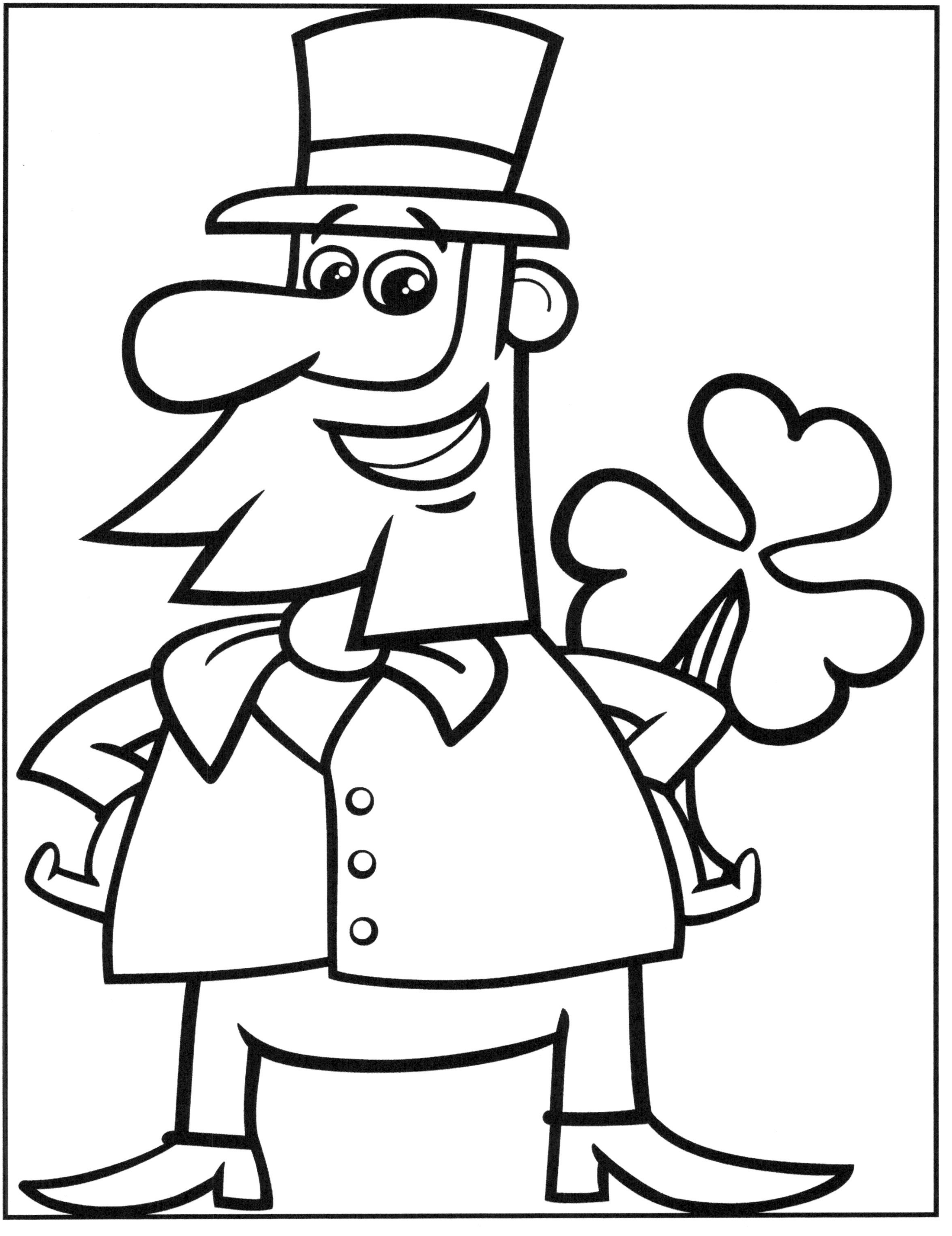

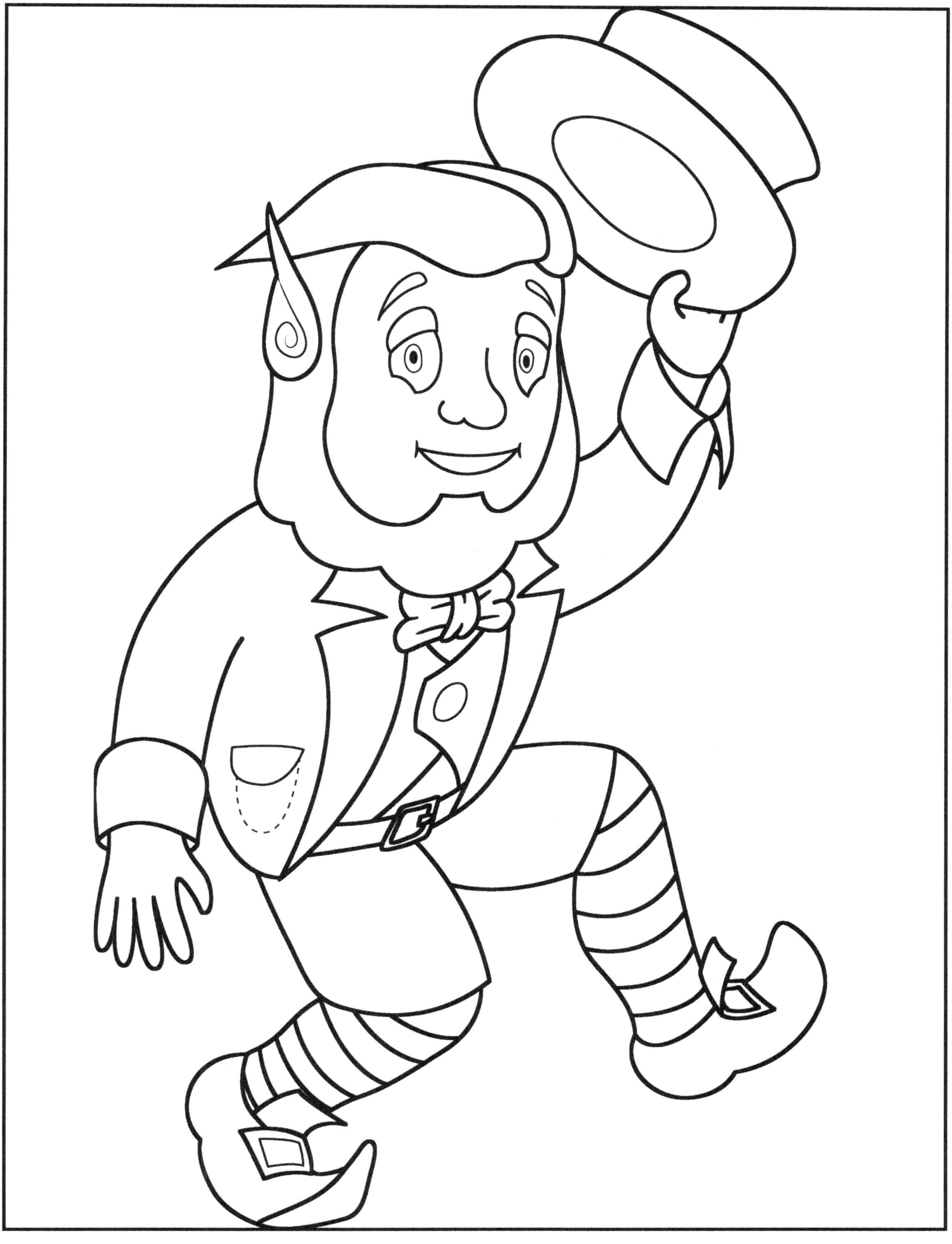

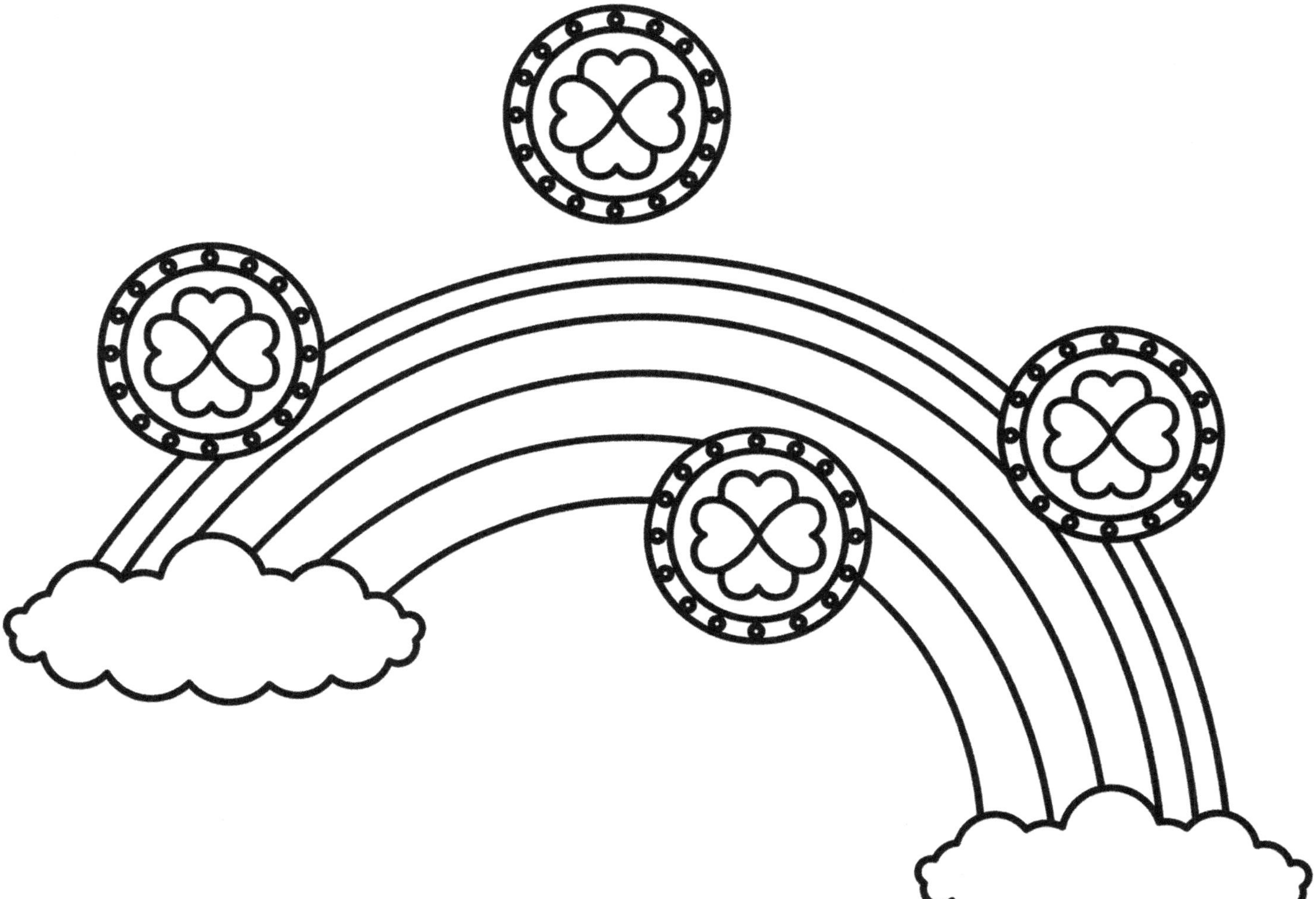

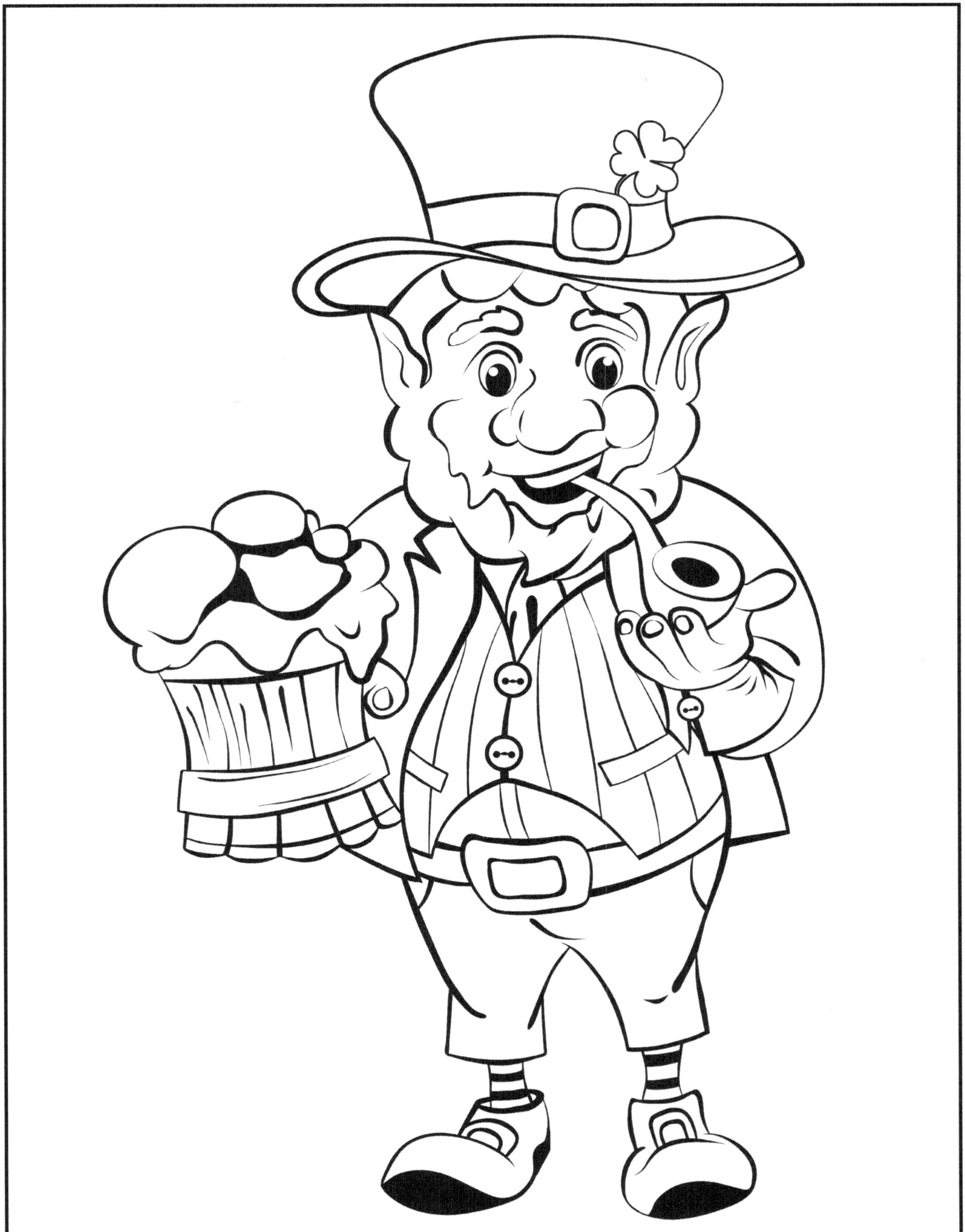

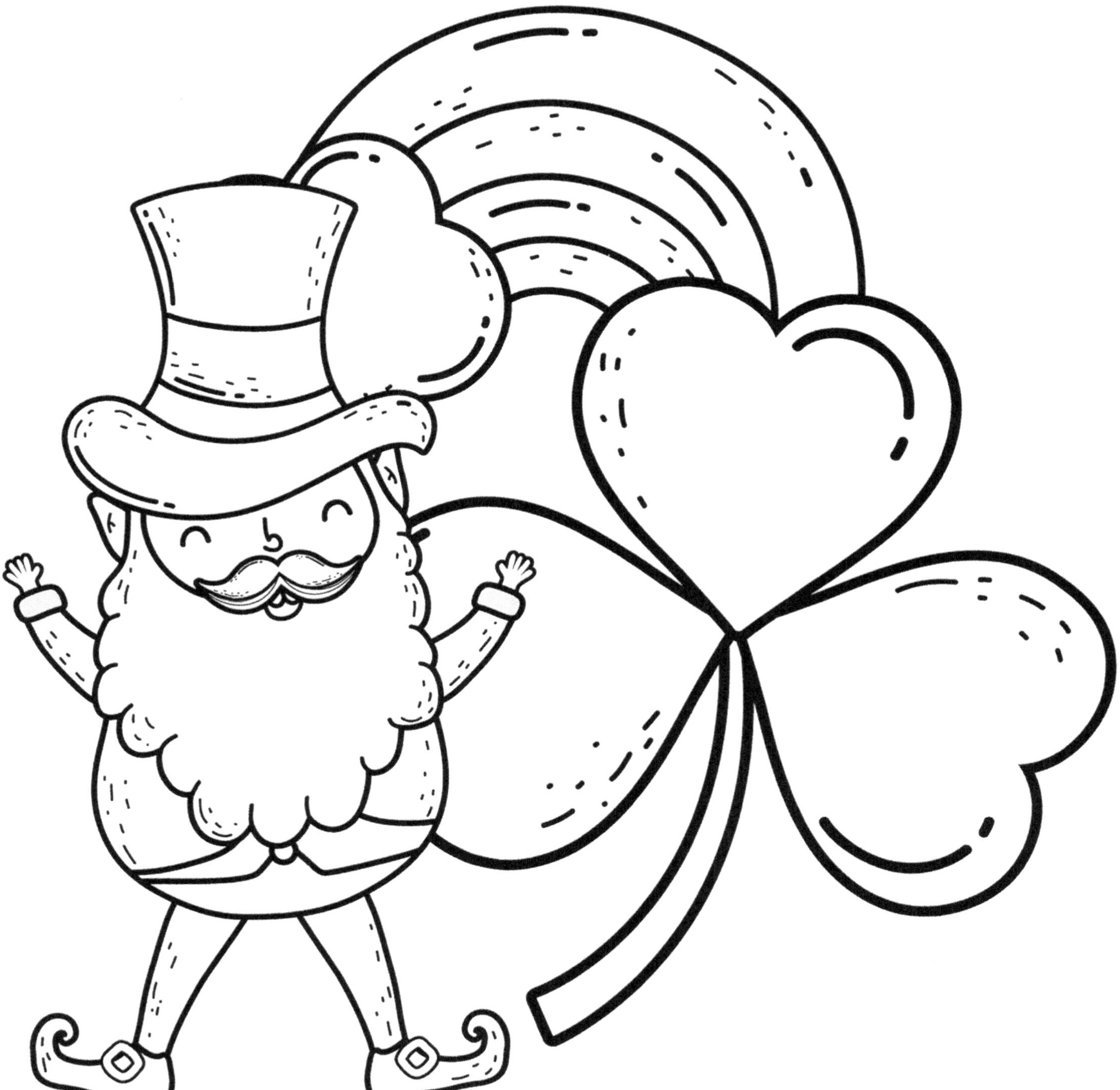

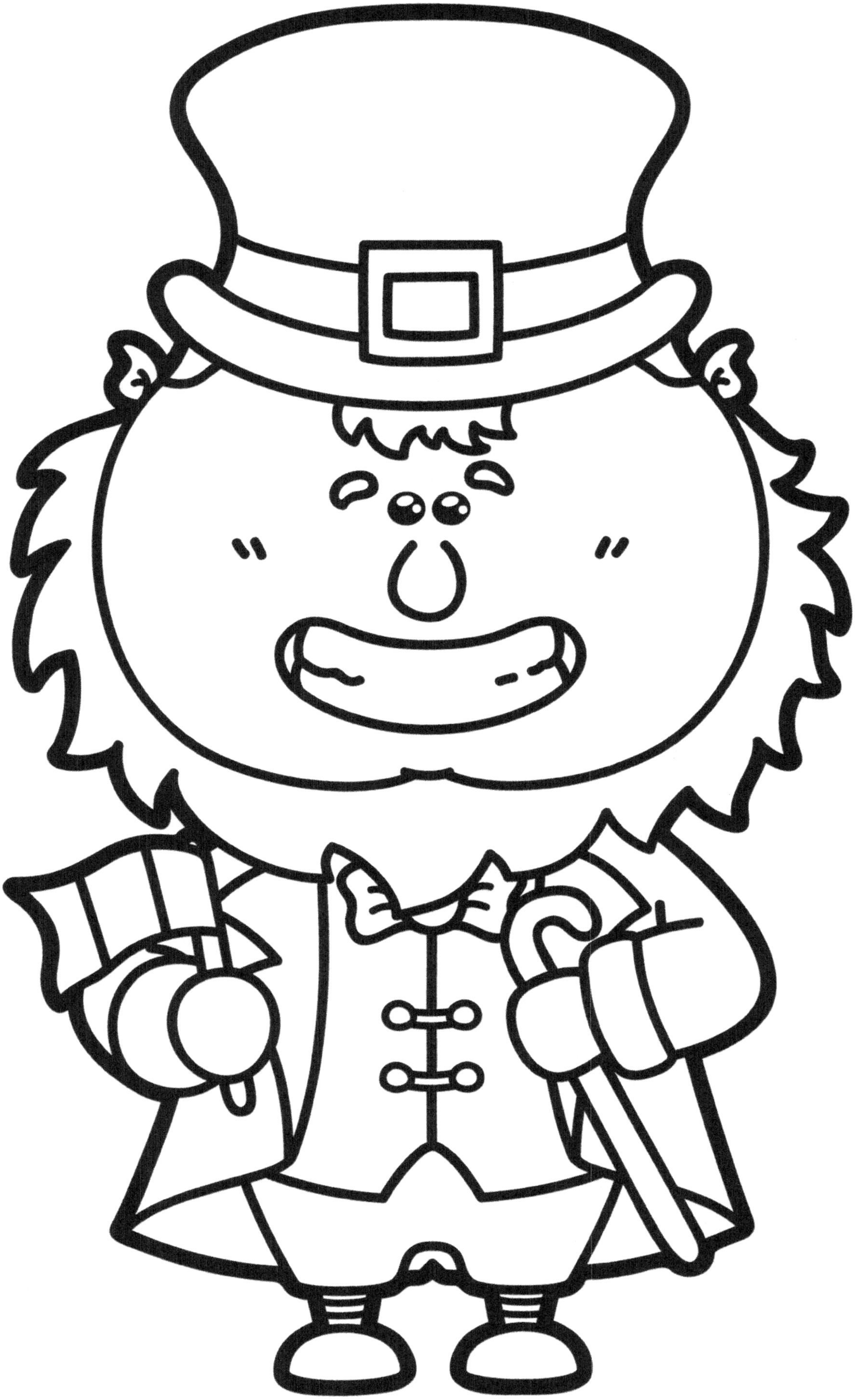

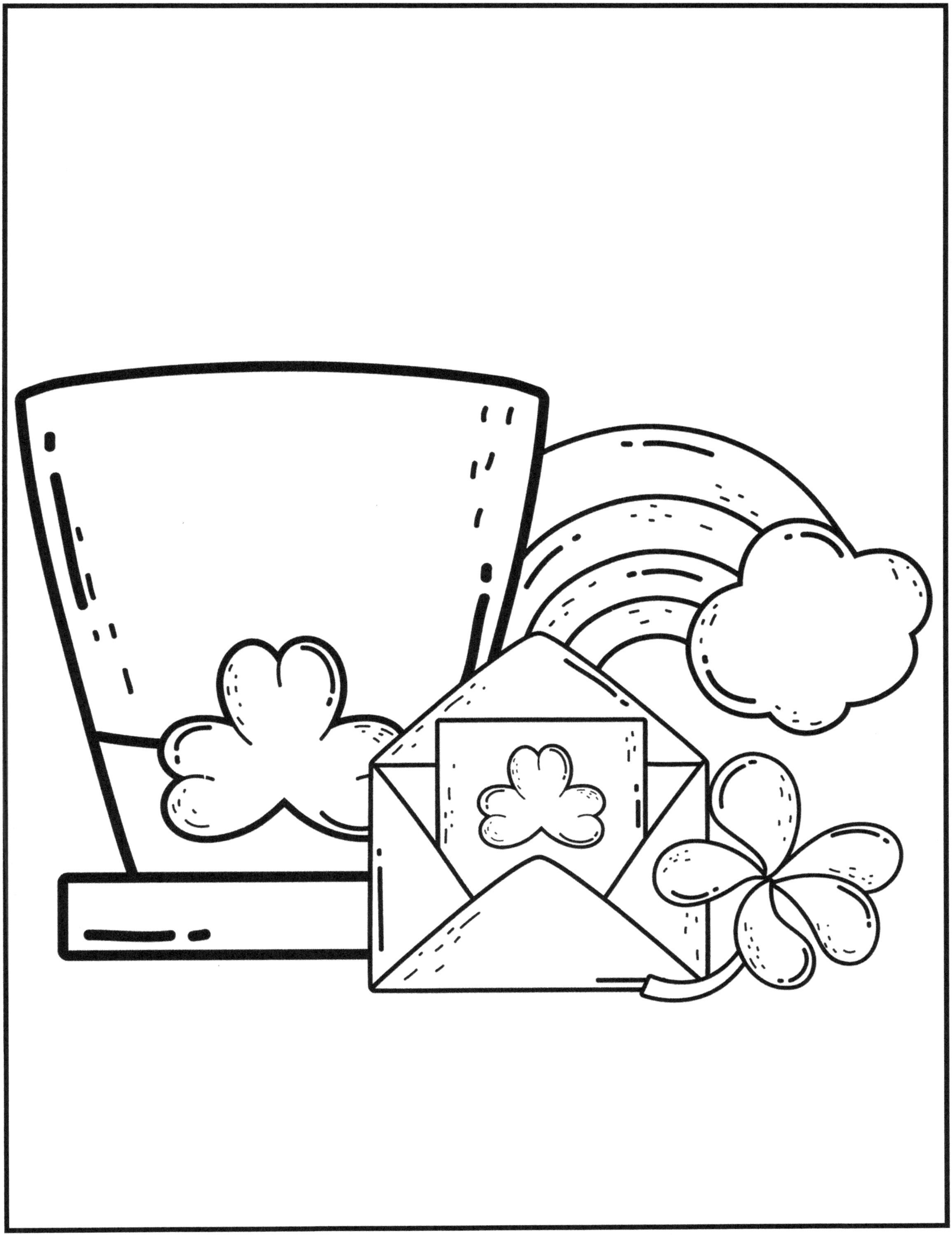

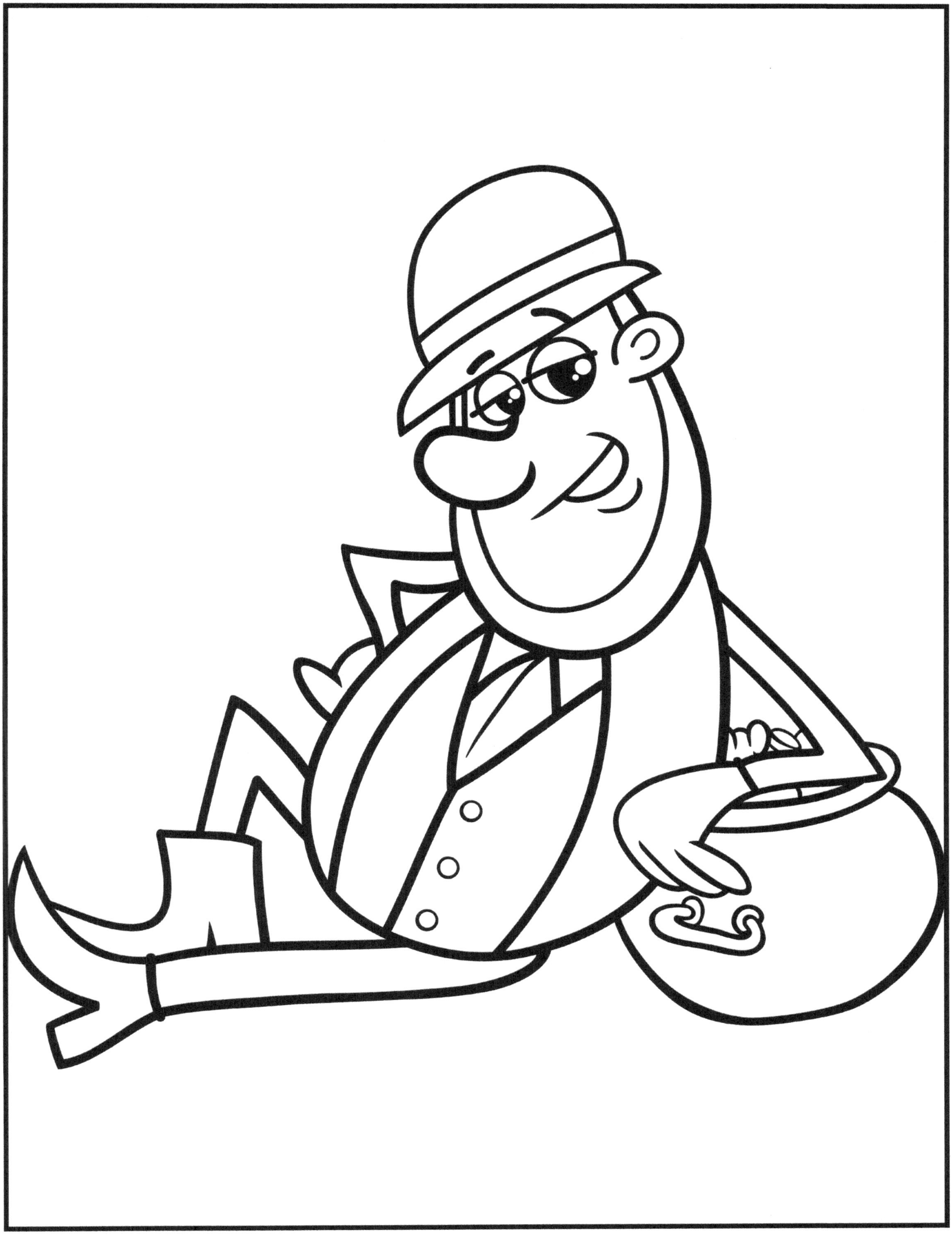

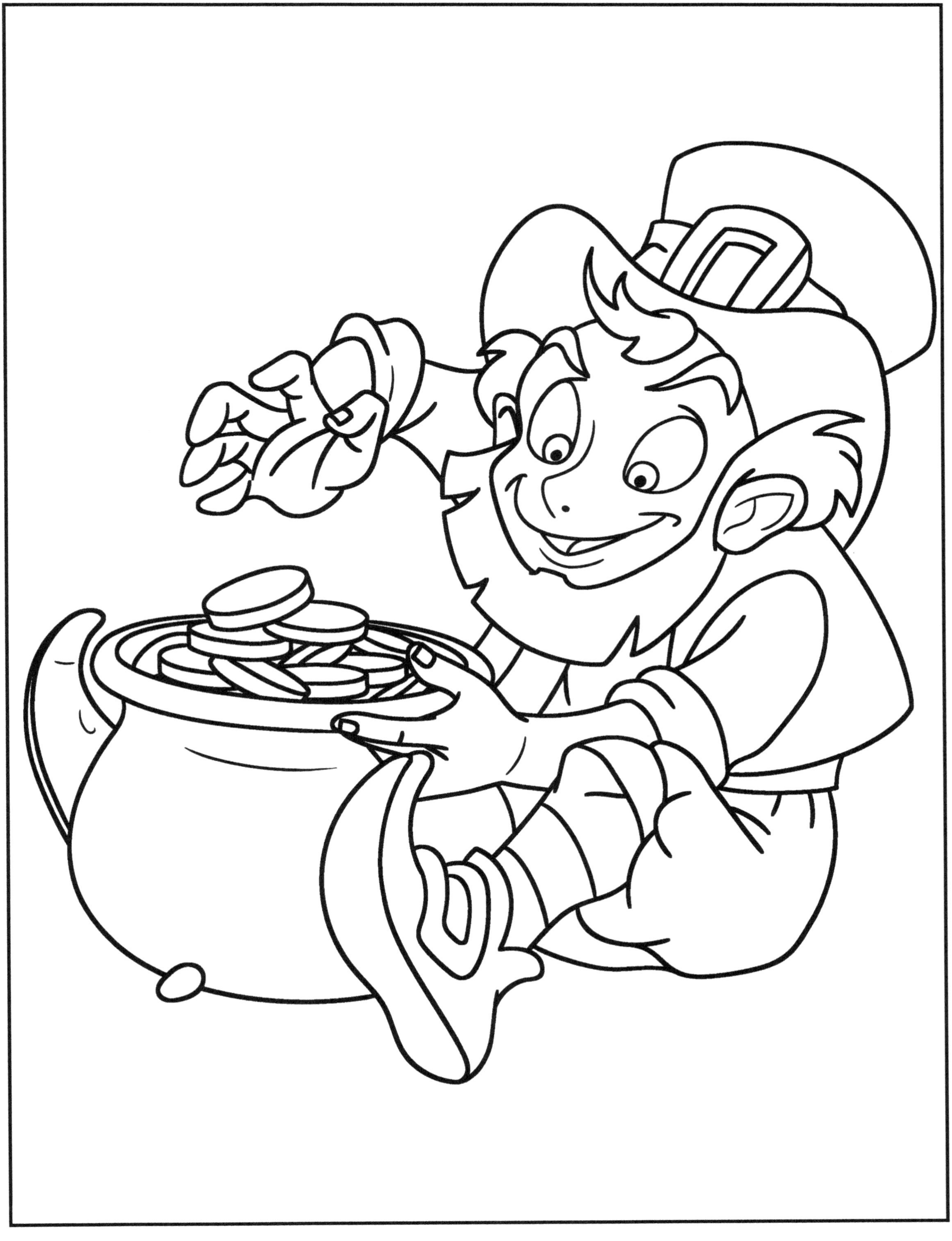

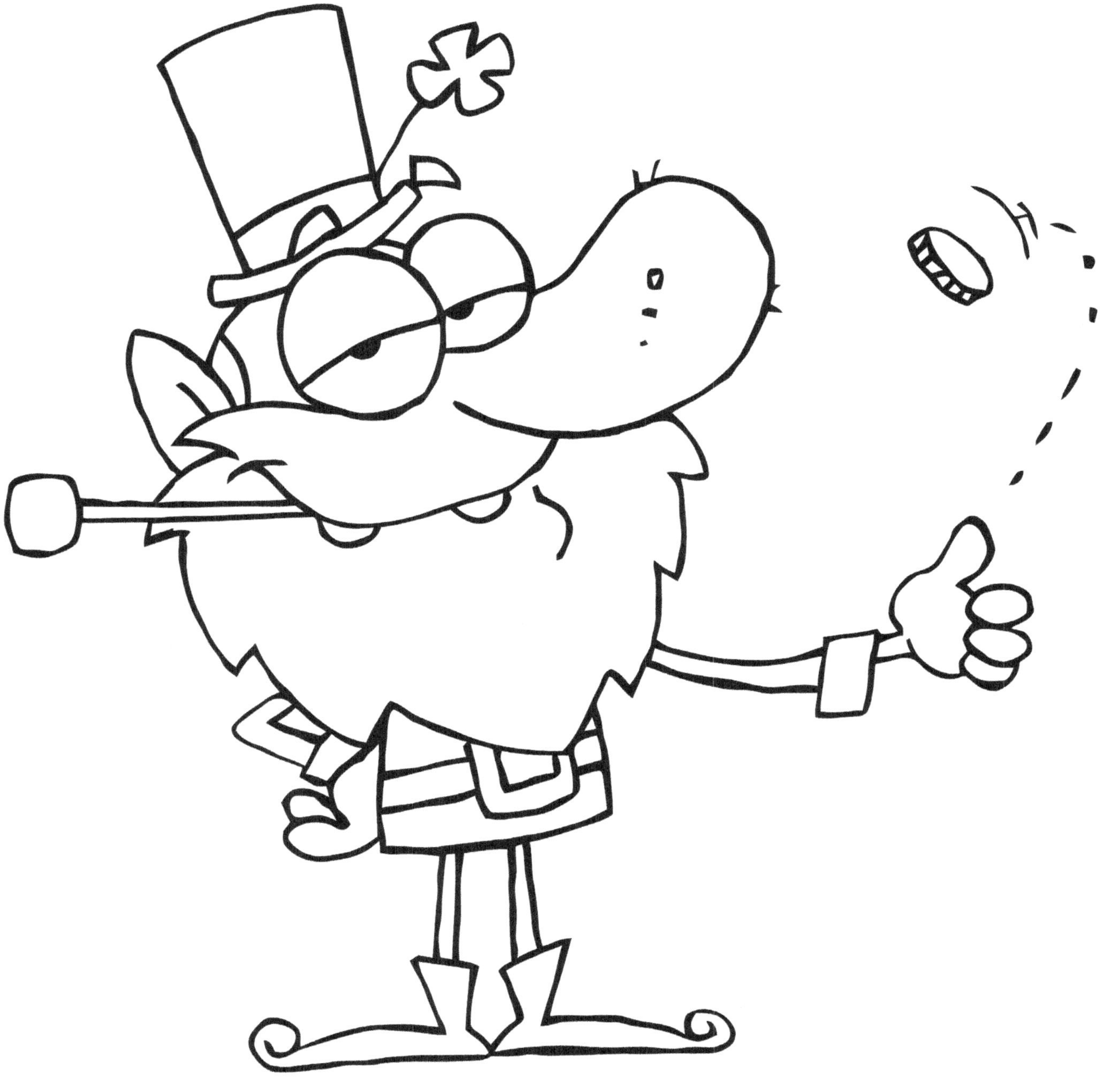

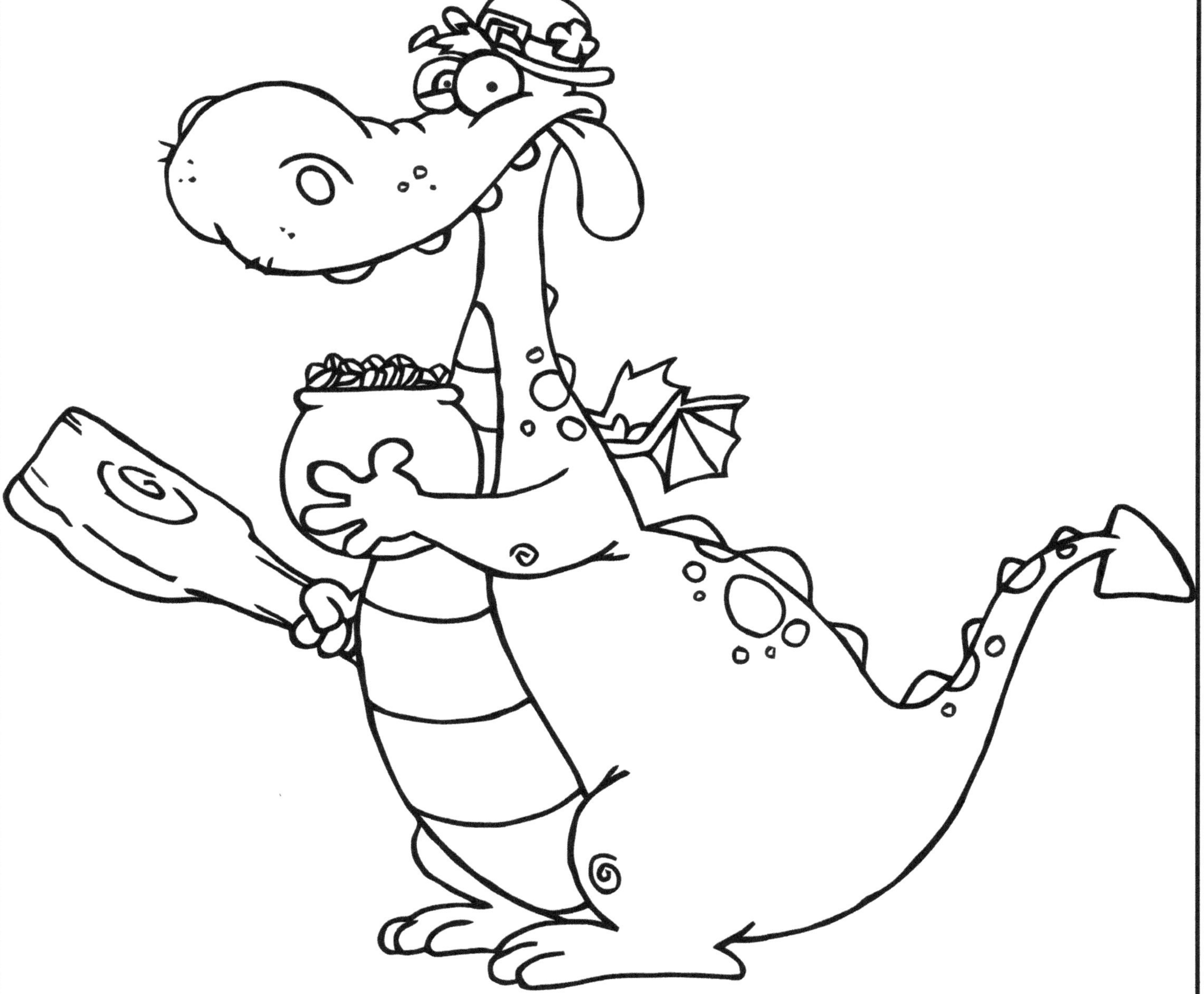

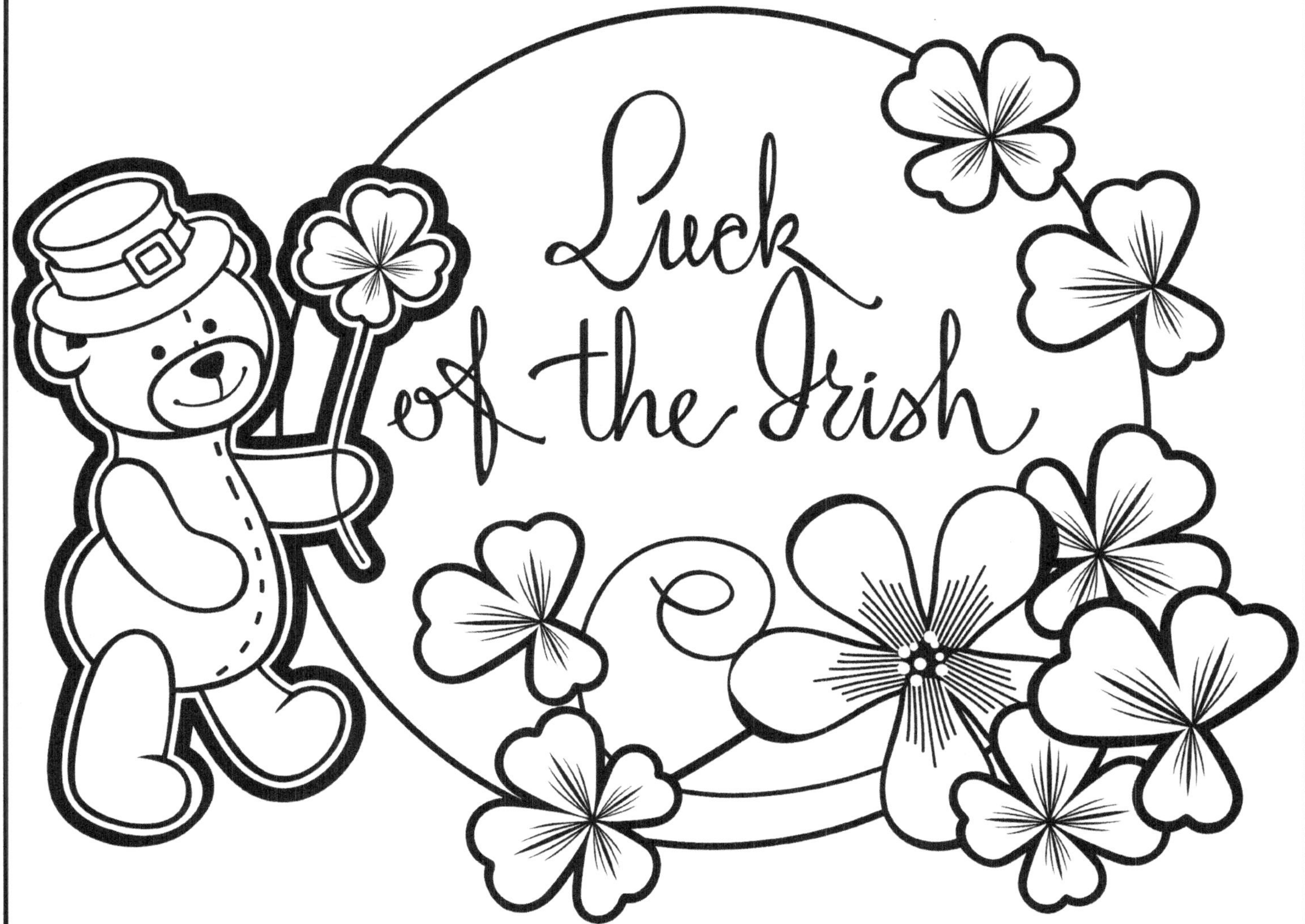
Luck
of the Irish

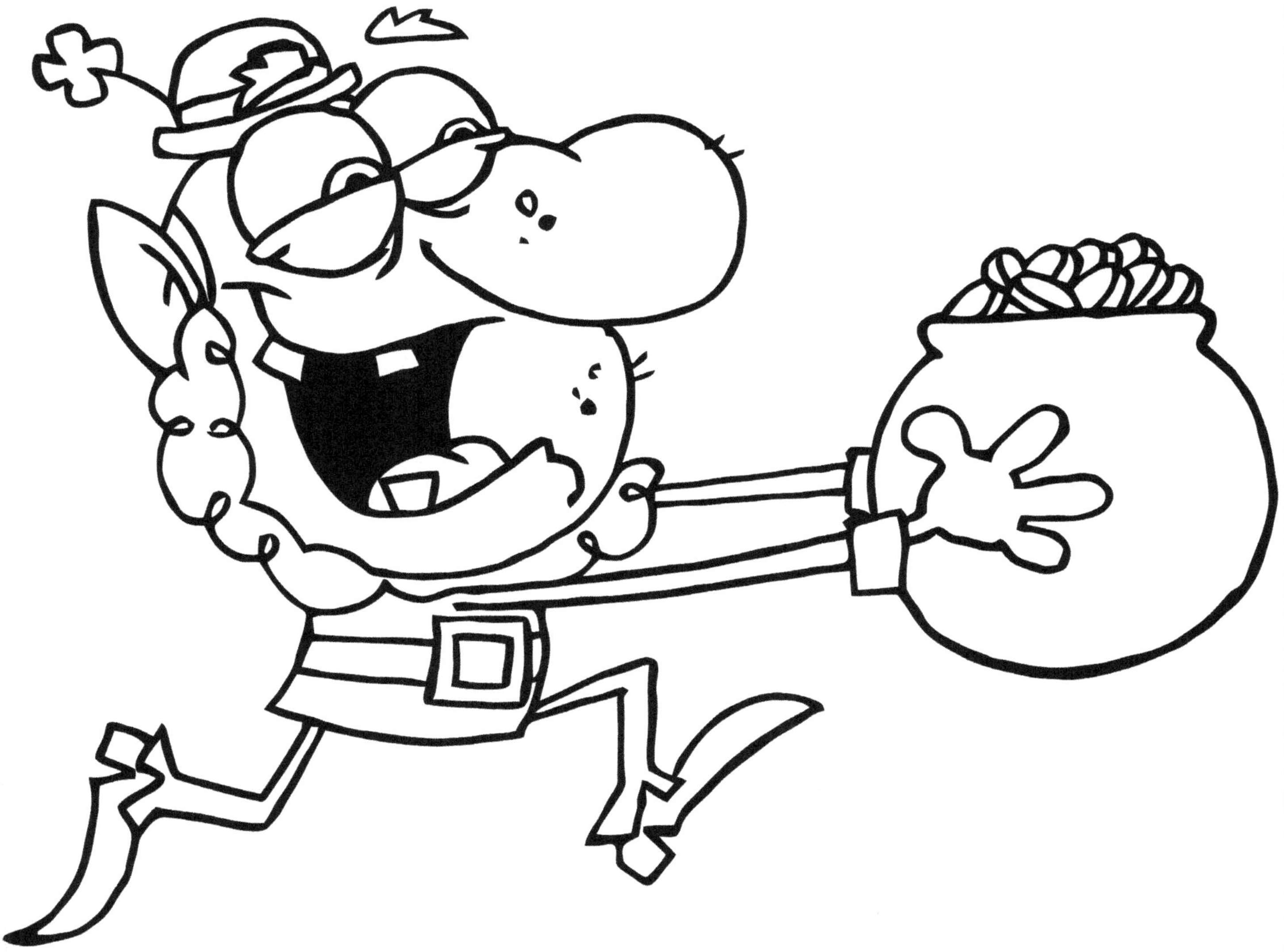

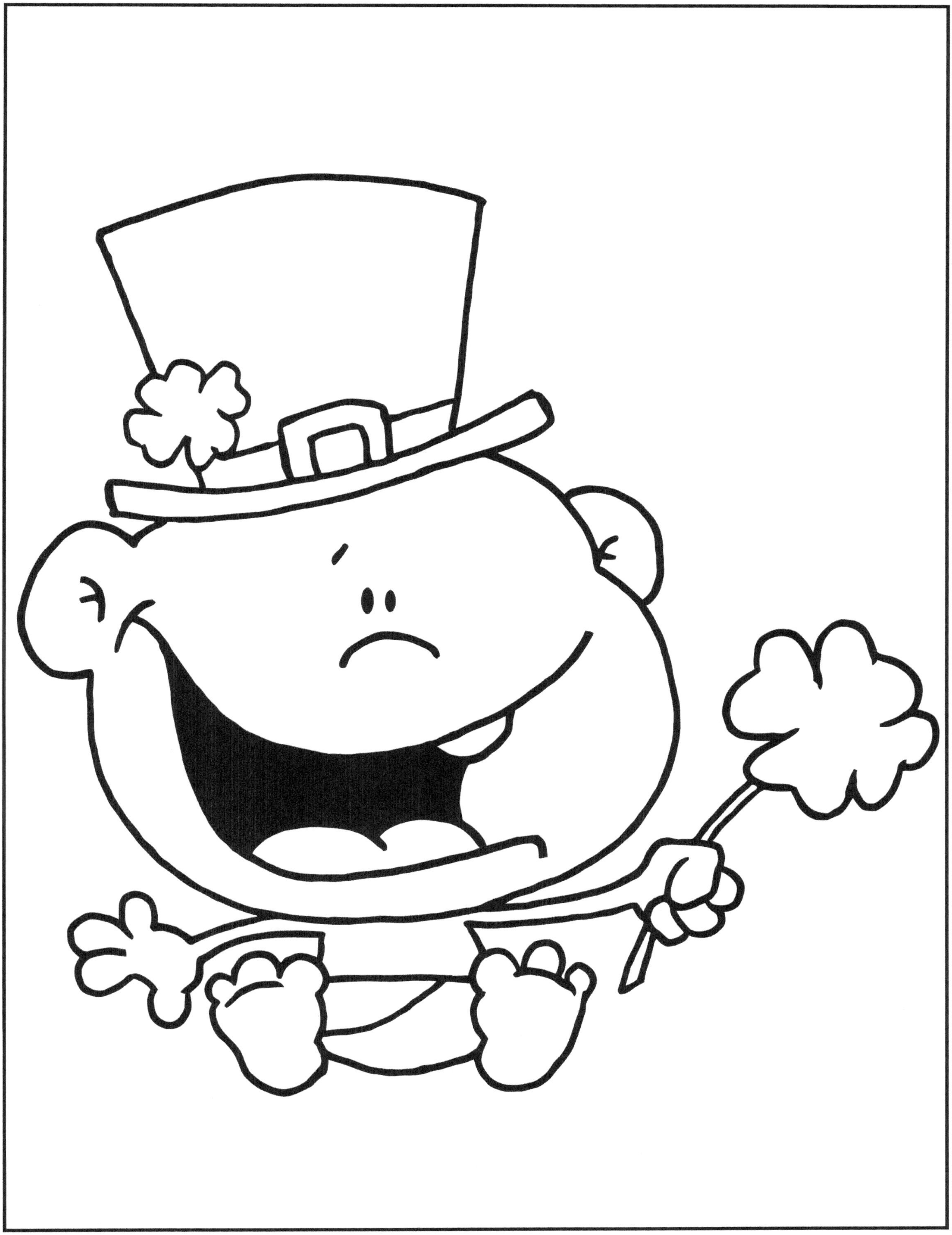

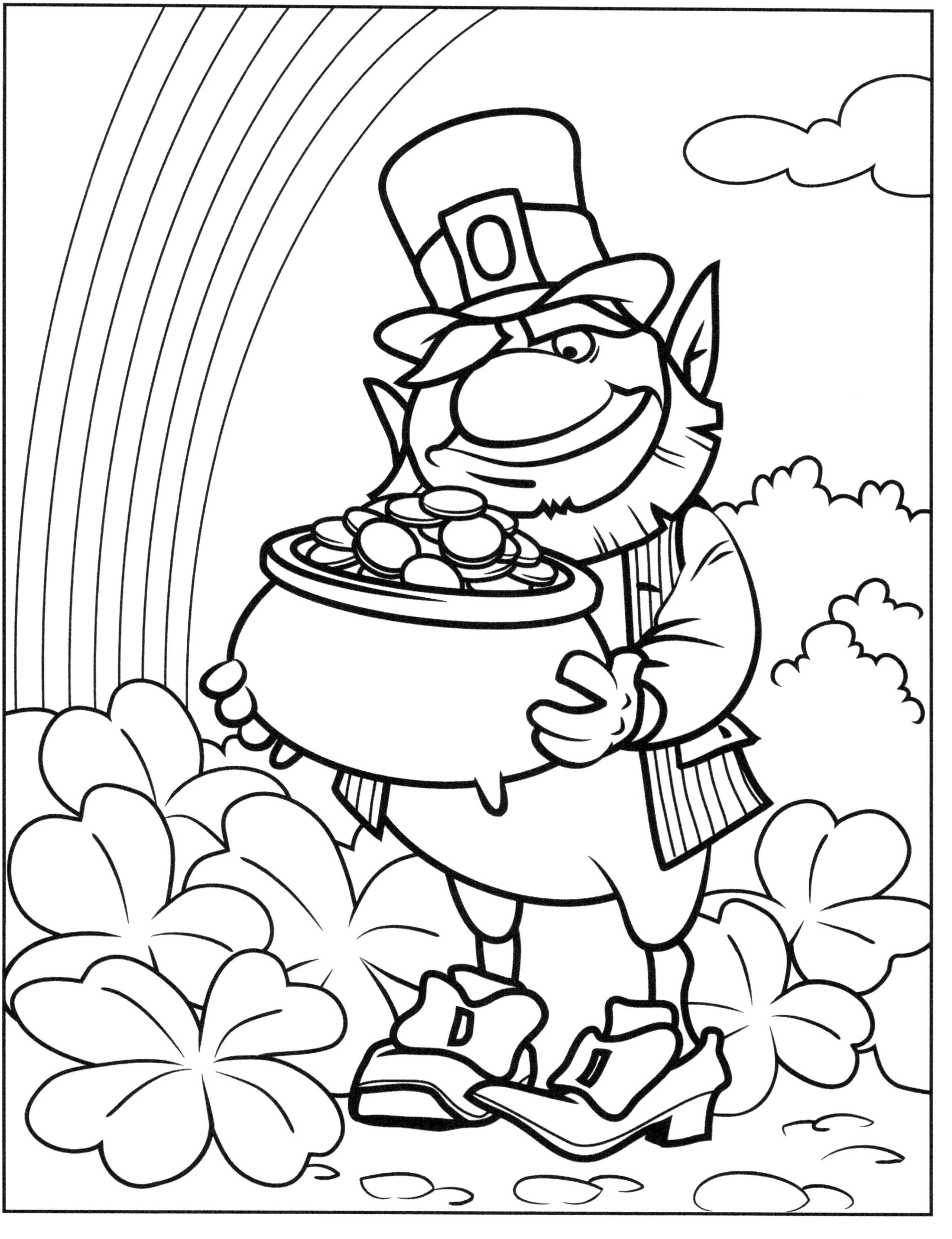

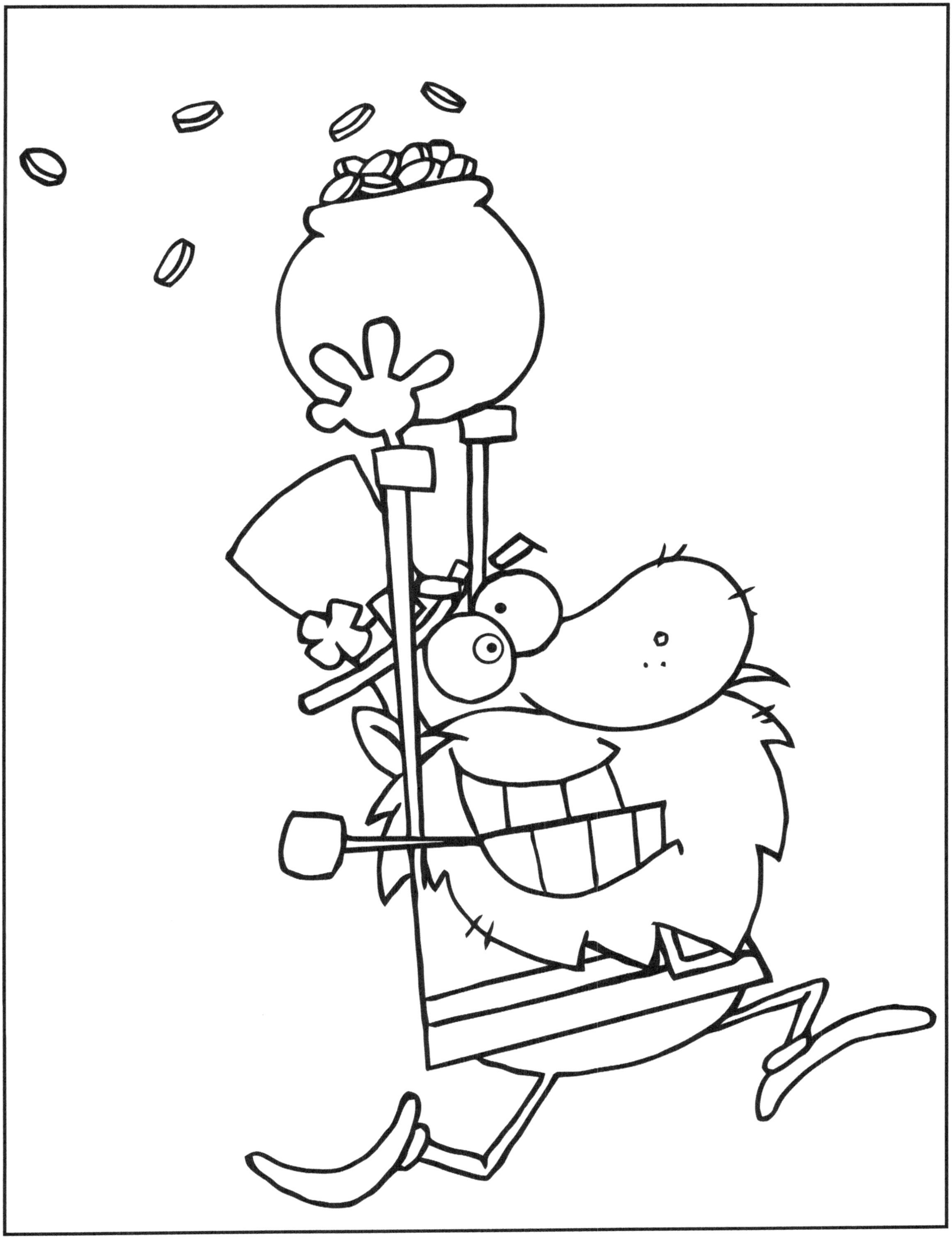

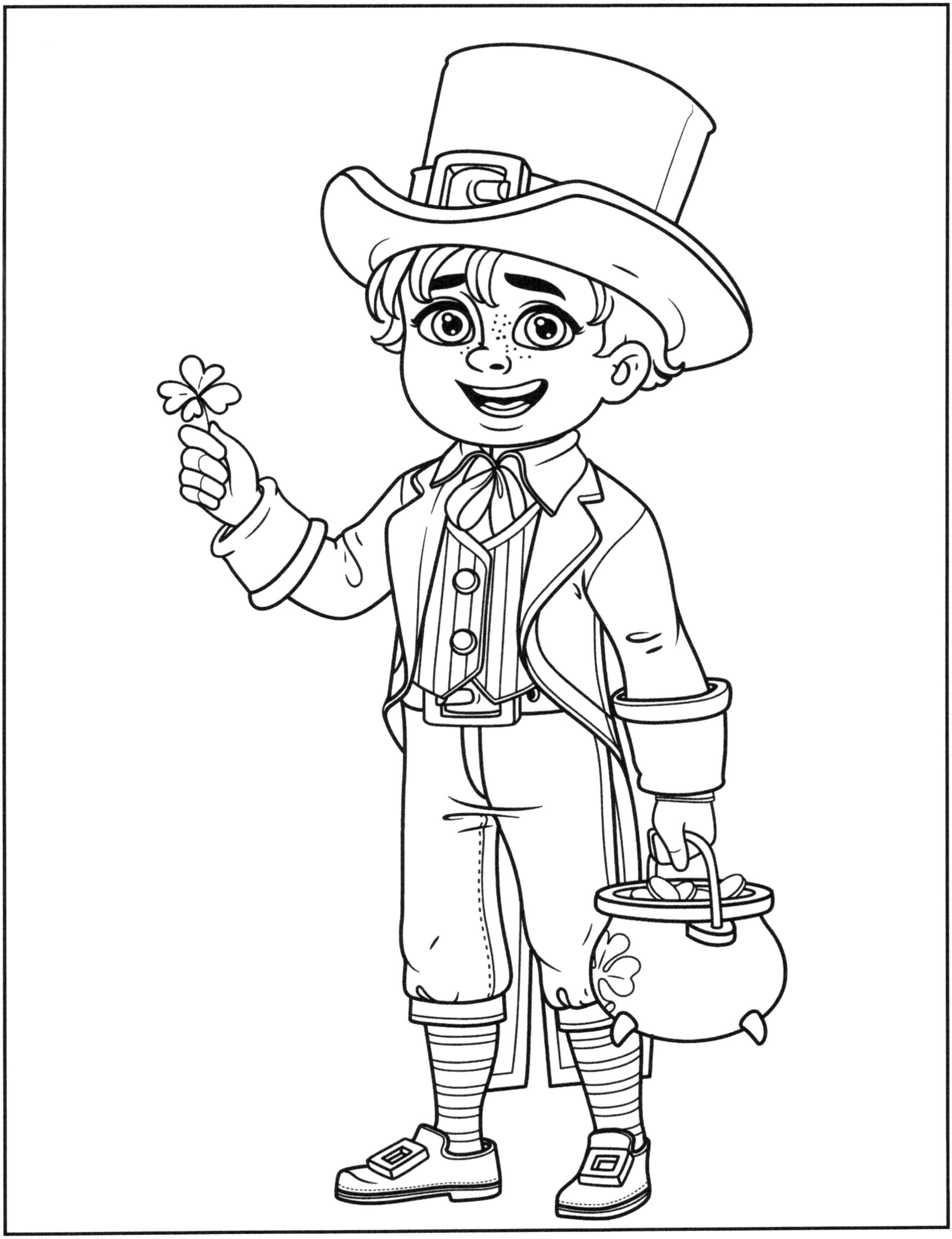

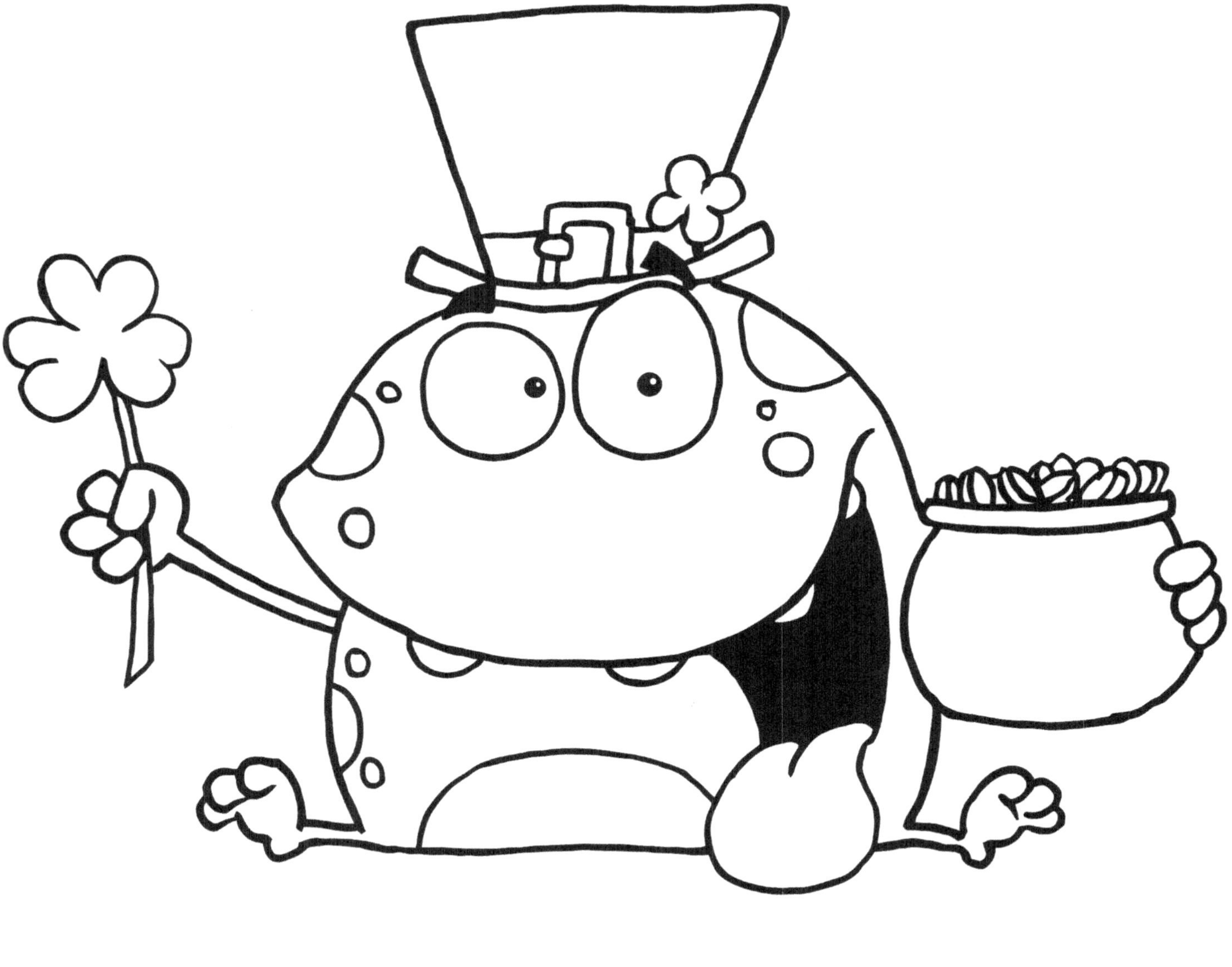

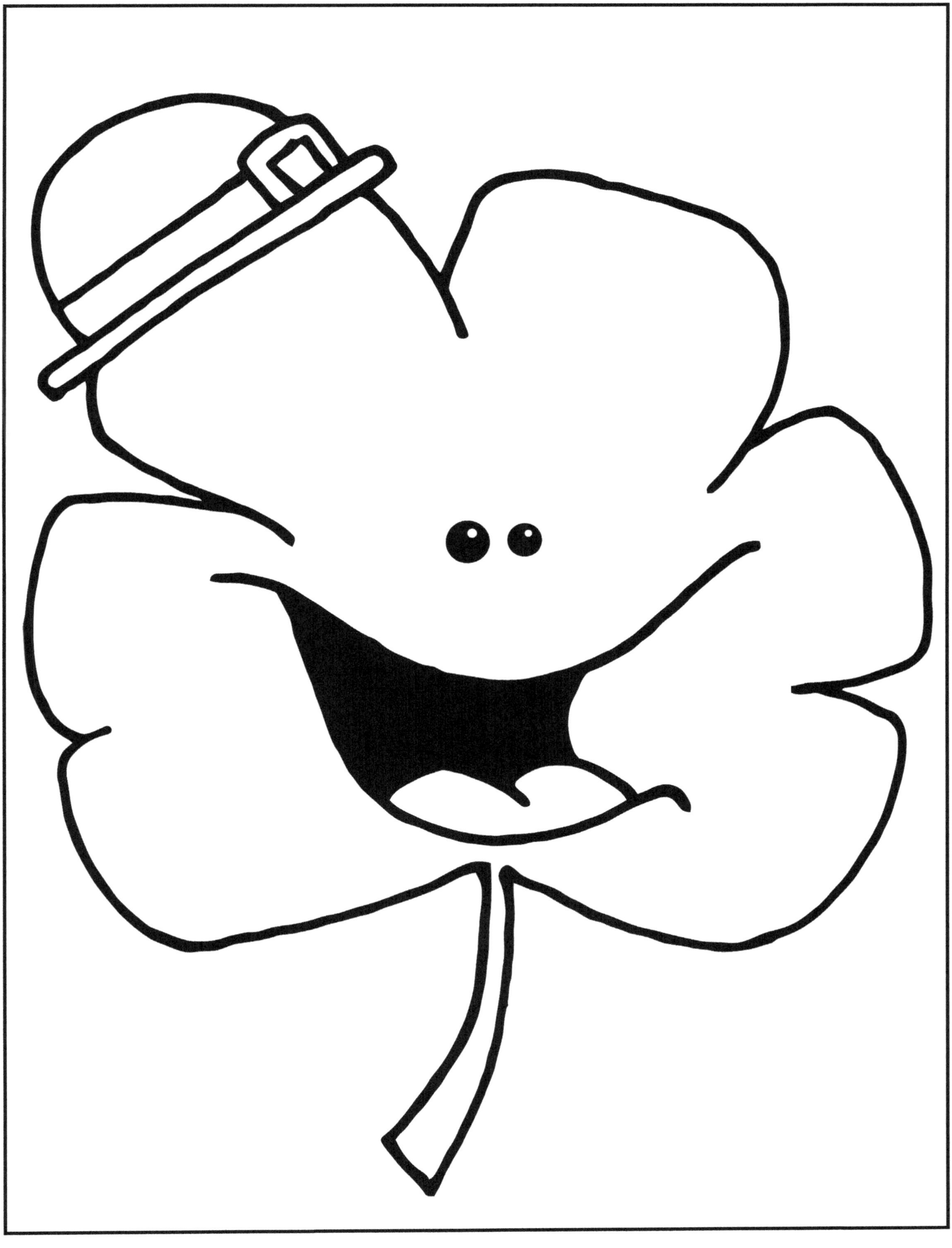

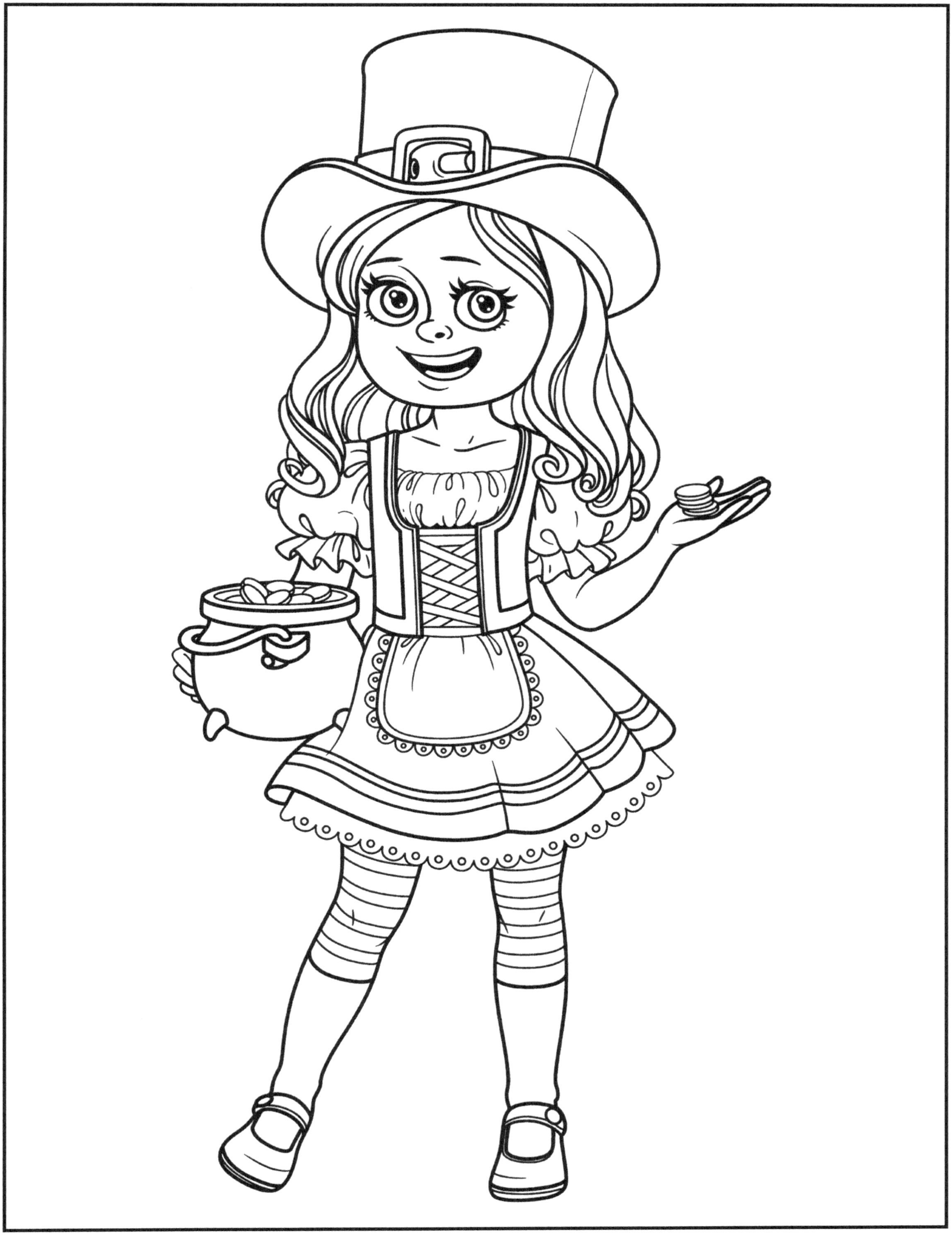

36569962R00040

Made in the USA
Middletown, DE
15 February 2019